Types of evidence:-

Photographic *evidence, pictures taken at the time under study, provide a rich source of information and detail. They often show the people who were involved in the making of history. This photograph, a still from the film* The Battle of the Somme, *shows men of the 29th Division (see p14-19) advancing into No Man's Land on July 1st 1916 at the start of the First Battle of the Somme. The Imperial War Museum (*IWM*) holds many such photographs for study. (Picture number* Q 79500*)*

Personal *recollections by those who were involved gives a unique and detailed reality to past events. Frank Bastable, now in his eighties, was on the Somme from mid-1915 until 1918 with the 7th Battalion Royal West Kent Regiment (see pages 10,20,28,30 and 40).*

Documentary evidence produced at the time under study sheds further light on the events. Poems, letters, and diaries come under this heading, as do newspaper reports and the Battalion War Diaries held by the Public Record Office at Kew. The newspaper report opposite and the 7th West Kent War Diary extract below refer to the death of Bill Beckington. Frank Bastable also told me about being with Bill when he was killed. Altogether the sad story individualises the tragedy of war (see p10-11).

Mr. and Mrs. Beckington received the following letter, which, although the news which it contains was so sad, no parent could read without a feeling of gratification:—

Dear Mrs. Beckington,—I am very sorry to have to tell you that your son was killed while in a working party on Wednesday, August 24th. He was in the front line trench within twenty yards of the enemy. I had known him for over a

By permission of the British Library; Newspaper Library.

Trenches 25/8/15 10.45 am Two men killed; shot in the head by bullets coming through the parapet.

(By permission of the Controller of H.M.S.O.; Public Record Office, ref. WO 95/2049)

Field *evidence is the most intriguing as its immediacy can stimulate an interest in, and understanding of, the past that other forms of evidence may not be able to do. The 'history that is around us' thus often provides the starting point for many historical studies. These are some British reserve trenches in Newfoundland Park. Men of 29th Div. advanced from here, and met their deaths, on July 1st 1916 (see p16-19). Cemeteries now mark the old front lines, providing a rather poignant form of field evidence. All the cemeteries have the Cross of Sacrifice.*

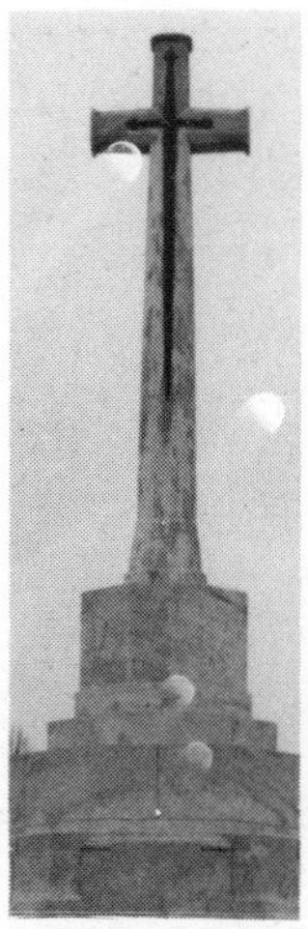

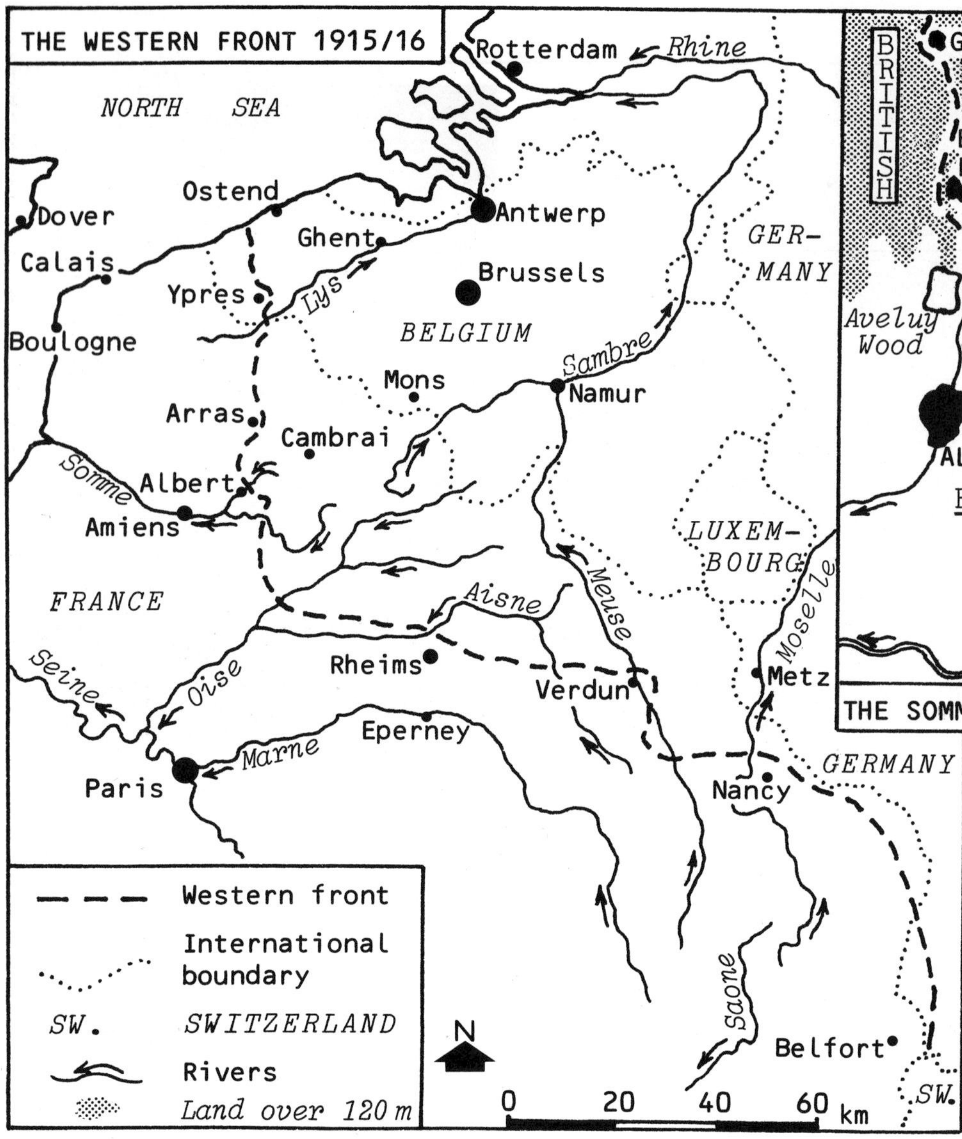

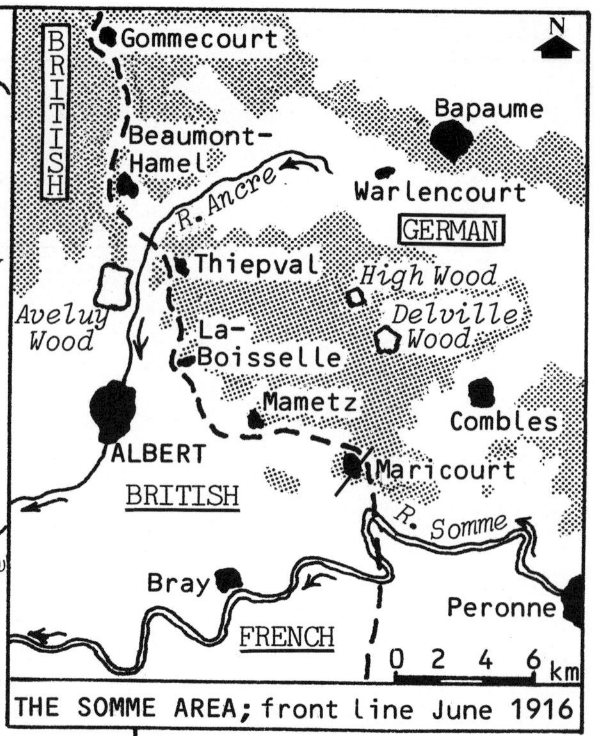

The Western Front: The war between Germany and the Allies (Britain, France and Russia) began on August 1st 1914. Germany invaded France -by way of Belgium - hoping to capture it before Britain could act. The German plan was then to turn their attention eastwards and capture Russia. Resolute action by French and British troops halted the German advance into France. The Germans retreated to the R.Aisne and then spread their forces to north and south in order to avoid being out-flanked. The result was that by the end of 1914 the two sides faced each other dug into parallel lines of trenches, called the Western Front, running from the Swiss border to the North Sea.

Throughout 1915 the Germans pressured to break the Allied front and reach the Channel ports. In mid-1915 Kitchener's 'New Army' of British and Empire volunteer soldiers landed in France via those very ports. One of the Western Front sectors they took over and held through to mid-1916 was the area just north of the river Somme in France. It was a 'quiet' sector during this time, but plans were being hatched by the Allied Commanders to change all that. But while the British and French were planning an attack, it was the Germans who actually did so, in Feb.1916 - against the French at Verdun.

To relieve the pressure on the French at Verdun a mainly British attack became a matter of some urgency. The original plan was for an equally shared effort, and later in the year to give Kitchener's 'New Army' time to train and prepare. The Somme sector of the Western Front was chosen for the 'Great Offensive' against the Germans. This meant that some of the attack would be by the French too because their sector joined the British one at Maricourt. So, despite the name 'Battle of the Somme' going down in British history, it was the French who actually attacked astride that river on July 1st 1916. The British effort on that day was directed towards pushing up the valleys and spurs leading up onto the wide chalk ridge which the Germans occupied north of the Somme river itself. This was known as Pozieres Ridge, and has been likened in appearance to Salisbury Plain. While not wishing to belittle the largely successful French effort on the Somme, this booklet concentrates on the British sector and the battles there between 1916 and 1918.

Cemeteries *mark the line of the old Western Front because the men were buried near where they fell in battle. Early in the war it was decided that the recording and burial of the dead should be done as thoroughly as possible. In May 1917 the Imperial War Graves Commission was set up to establish and maintain British and Empire military cemeteries (renamed Commonwealth W.G.C. in 1960). These peaceful and beautiful cemeteries, each one named, have a number of features in common. Every one has a Cross of Sacrifice and the larger ones a Stone of Remembrance, both in white Portland stone. The headstones are uniform in size and shape - reminding one of ranks of soldiers - and each one carries the name of the soldier, his rank, regiment, the date he died, and often his age and an inscription chosen by his relatives. Headstones of unknown soldiers are inscribed* A Soldier of the Great War *and* Known Unto God, *words chosen by Rudyard Kipling who himself lost a son in the war.*

The cemeteries provide a poignant form of field evidence today. Their very location on the old battle lines, as well as the details on the headstones and in the Cemetery Registers found at most of them, record the place and times at which events occurred. The cemeteries thus 'freeze' the action for us and, at the same time, provide us with details of the men involved. Such details obtained through field visits to France can start a search for other types of evidence at home in order to build a fuller picture of events or individuals. This was the case with Lt.Henry Webber, whose headstone in the Dartmoor Cemetery, Becordel (see 23 on map p6) interested me because of his age and because Horley is near my own home.

Serre Road Cemetery №2 at 5 on map page 6.

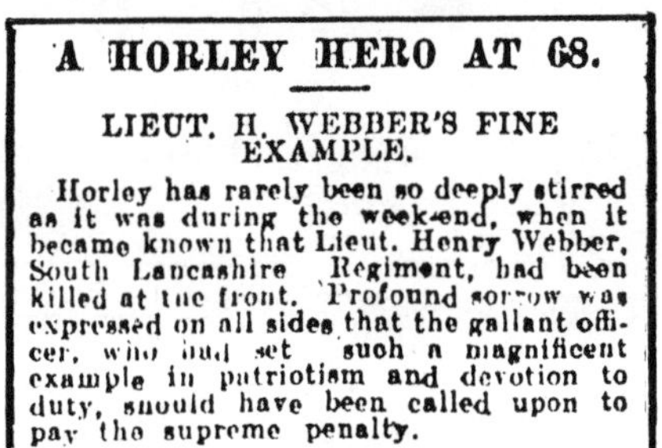

A HORLEY HERO AT 68.

LIEUT. H. WEBBER'S FINE EXAMPLE.

Horley has rarely been so deeply stirred as it was during the week-end, when it became known that Lieut. Henry Webber, South Lancashire Regiment, had been killed at the front. Profound sorrow was expressed on all sides that the gallant officer, who had set such a magnificent example in patriotism and devotion to duty, should have been called upon to pay the supreme penalty.

By the permission of the British Library;Newspaper Library, London.

Lt.Henry Webber's *headstone at Becordel led me to visit Horley's War Memorial where I saw his name, and then to read about this much respected man in the* Horley Advertiser *for Aug.5th 1916. He was the oldest British soldier to die on the Western Front, insisting on going to the war despite his age. His story was thus revealed by moving from field to documentary evidence.*

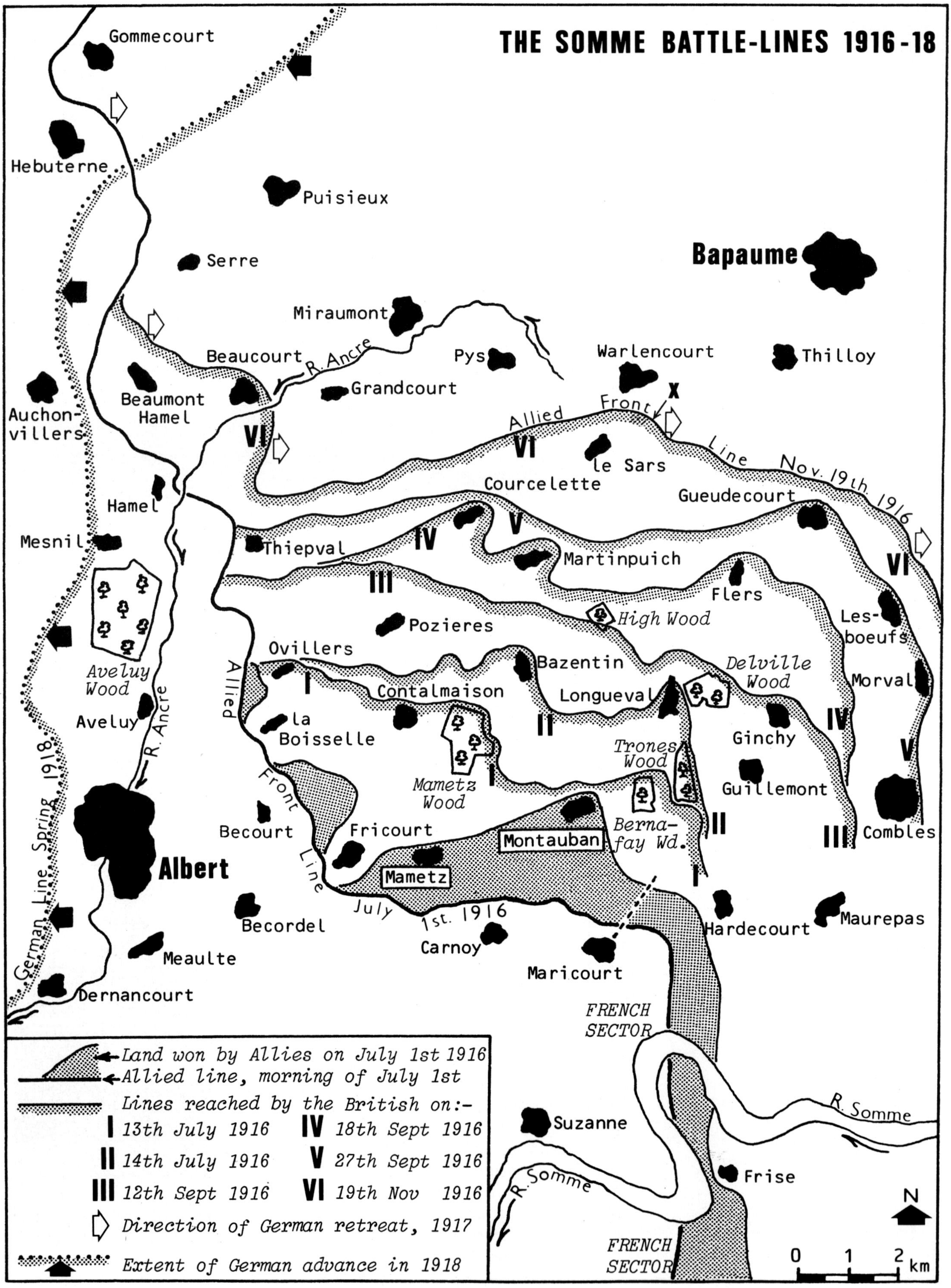

THE SOMME BATTLE-LINES 1916-18
Gommecourt
Hebuterne
Puisieux
Serre
Bapaume
Miraumont
Beaucourt
R. Ancre
Pys
Warlencourt
Thilloy
Grandcourt
Beaumont Hamel
Auchonvillers
Allied Front Line Nov. 19th 1916
X
VI
le Sars
Courcelette
Gueudecourt
Hamel
Mesnil
Thiepval
IV
V
Martinpuich
III
Flers
Lesboeufs
High Wood
Pozieres
Ovillers
Bazentin
Delville Wood
Morval
Aveluy Wood
Contalmaison
Longueval
I
II
Aveluy
la Boisselle
Ginchy
Allied Front Line July 1st. 1916
Trones Wood
Mametz Wood
Guillemont
Becourt
Fricourt
Montauban
Bernafay Wd.
Combles
Albert
Mametz
German Line Spring 1918
Becordel
Carnoy
Hardecourt
Maurepas
Meaulte
Maricourt
Dernancourt
FRENCH SECTOR
Land won by Allies on July 1st 1916
Allied line, morning of July 1st
Lines reached by the British on:-
I 13th July 1916
II 14th July 1916
III 12th Sept 1916
IV 18th Sept 1916
V 27th Sept 1916
VI 19th Nov 1916
Direction of German retreat, 1917
Extent of German advance in 1918
R. Somme
Suzanne
Frise
N
0 1 2 km

The Somme Battles 1916-1918:-

'First Somme', 1916: The line held by the British from mid-1915 (see p10) is that shown for the morning of July 1st 1916. The British held the land to the west, while the Germans held the land to the east of the line. The first Allied Offensive on the Somme began with a preliminary bombardment lasting a week (p12), the infantry attack beginning at 7.30 a.m. on July 1st 1916. The plan was to take the German front line and all their fortified villages from Serre to Montauban on July 1st, and then to attack their Second Line of Defences before finally breaking through to Bapaume and beyond - all in a matter of days. However, very little was achieved on July 1st, especially from Fricourt northwards. There was little to show for the 21,000 British soldiers who died that day (see pages 14-29 for details of each sector on July 1st).

As most initial success was in the southern area on July 1st, more effort was expended there as the battle progressed, resulting in the original objectives for that day being reached by July 13th (line I), but with little progress in the north. The Second Line of German Defences was attacked, again in the south only, on July 13/14th, including an attack on Trones Wood (p30: line II). The struggle for Pozieres Ridge, including the battle for Delville Wood (p32), lasted until mid-September (line III). Tanks were used for the first time ever in the attack on Flers, Courcelette and High Wood on Sept.15th (p34: line IV). Thiepval and Beaumont Hamel were not taken until Sept.27th (p21: line V) and Nov.13th (p18: line VI) respectively. The extreme northern area, from Serre to Gommecourt, did not fall into British hands until the German withdrawal in 1917. 'First Somme' drew to an indecisive close amidst the mud and misery of the winter on Nov.19th 1916 (line VI). During the three and a half months of the battle the casualties, taking both sides, exceeded a million.

The Butte de Warlencourt *(see x on map) was on the final line of 'First Somme' in Nov.1916.*

1917; German retreat: *Although indecisive, 'First Somme' exhausted the German forces in 1916. Fearing they might not be able to hold on in 1917, the Germans prepared a strong 'fall-back' line of defences about 15 km east of their 1916 lines called the* Hindenburg Line. *The Germans began to retreat to this line in Feb. 1917 (p36), a tactical move of consolidation by them, not an Allied victory as some claimed at the time.*

German advance and 'Second Somme', 1918: *The Allies planned to attack the Hindenburg Line in spring 1918, but it was the Germans who attacked first. Hordes of Germans emerged from the morning fog on March 21st 1918, and in just ten days advanced westwards across the old Somme battlefield and beyond (see map opposite and p36-37). However, the Germans were eventually halted just east of Amiens, and by the summer of 1918 it was the Allies' turn to launch an offensive. Beginning on August 8th, they pushed forward, across the old Somme battlefield yet again (p38), until the Germans eventually agreed to an end to the war, or at least an armistice, on November 11th 1918.*

A Demarcation Stone at Villers Bretonneux (see map p36) set up to mark the furthest extent of the German advance in spring 1918.

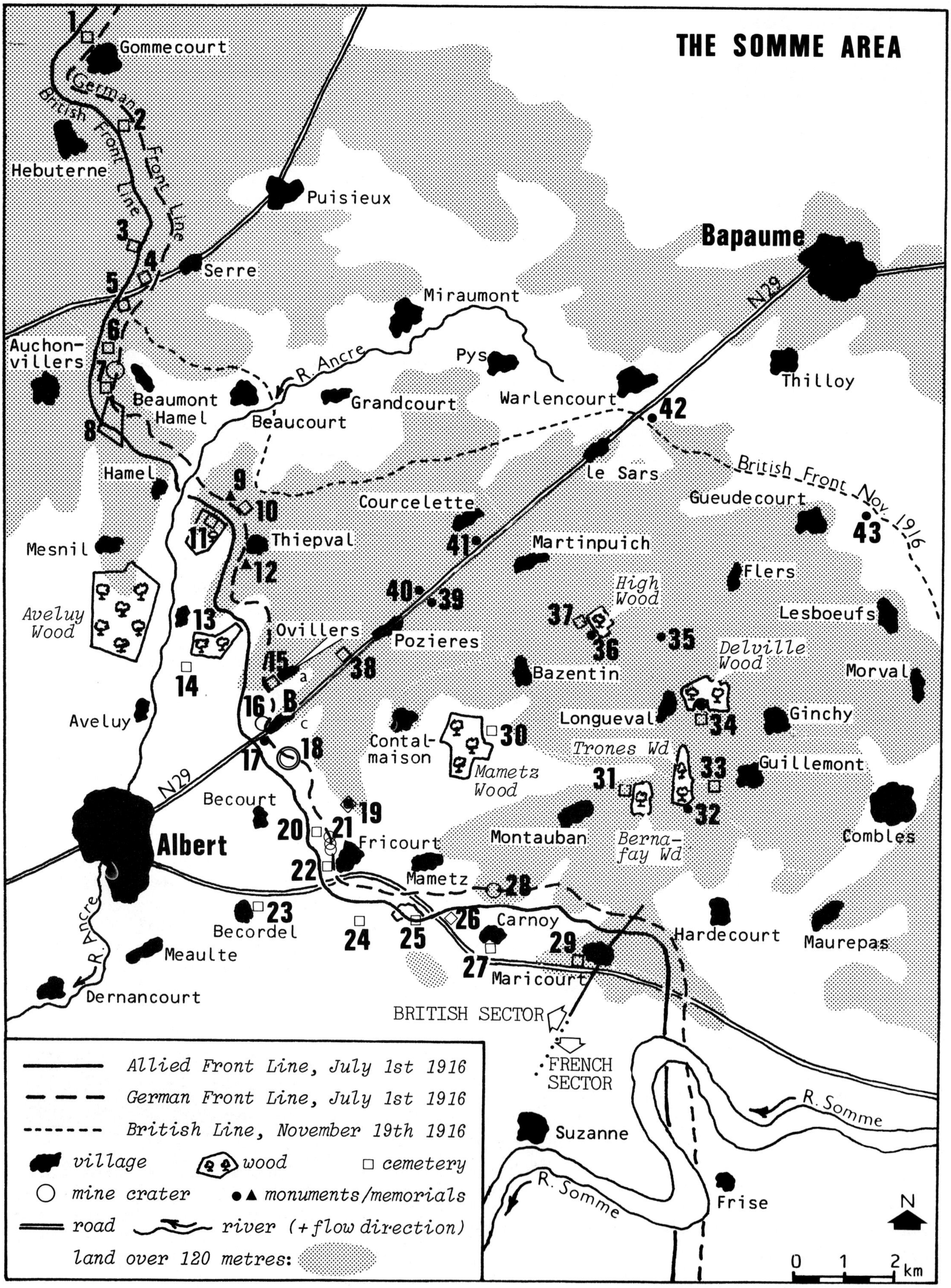
THE SOMME AREA
Gommecourt
German Front Line
British Front Line
Hebuterne
Puisieux
Bapaume
Serre
Miraumont
Auchonvillers
R. Ancre
Pys
Thilloy
Beaumont Hamel
Grandcourt
Warlencourt
Beaucourt
Hamel
Le Sars
British Front Nov. 1916
Courcelette
Gueudecourt
Thiepval
Mesnil
Martinpuich
Flers
High Wood
Aveluy Wood
Lesboeufs
Ovillers
Pozieres
Delville Wood
Bazentin
Morval
Aveluy
Longueval
Ginchy
Contalmaison
Trones Wd
Guillemont
Mametz Wood
Becourt
Albert
Fricourt
Montauban
Bernafay Wd
Combles
Mametz
Carnoy
Becordel
Hardecourt
Maurepas
Meaulte
Maricourt
Dernancourt
N29
BRITISH SECTOR
FRENCH SECTOR
Suzanne
R. Somme
Frise
N
0 1 2 km
Allied Front Line, July 1st 1916
German Front Line, July 1st 1916
British Line, November 19th 1916
village
wood
cemetery
mine crater
monuments/memorials
road
river (+flow direction)
land over 120 metres:

The Memorial to the Missing, Thiepval, *is a tall and impressive building. Standing as it does on the heights of the Pozieres Ridge (see* 12 *on map) it is visible from many places in the Somme battlefield area. The Memorial commemorates the "Officers and Men who fought on the Somme July 1915 to Feb 1918, but who have no known graves". The names of over 73,000 such men are carved into stone panels on the inside walls. The Memorial is also dedicated to the French and, to further signify the Anglo-French collaboration in the Somme battles, a small cemetery near the Memorial has an equal number of French and British graves. The Memorial stands on the site of the Thiepval Chateau which, although attacked by the British on July 1st, was not taken until late September 1916.*

Key: The suggested field study sites on the map opposite relate principally to the places and events mentioned in this booklet. The numbering of the sites on the map follows the plan of the major part of the booklet, i.e. tracing the front line of July 1st 1916 from north to south, then moving into the area of subsequent fighting up to Nov. 1916.

1 *Gommecourt Wood New Cemetery*
2 *Gommecourt British Cemetery No. 2*
3 *Sheffield Park and Railway Hollow Cem.*
4 *Serre Road Cemetery No. 1*
5 *Serre Road Cemetery No. 2*
6 *Beaumont Hamel British Cemetery*
7 *Hawthorn Mine Crater and Hawthorn Ridge Cemetery No. 1*
8 *The Newfoundland Memorial Park*
9 *The Ulster Tower*
10 *Mill Road Cemetery/Schwaben Redoubt*
11 *Thiepval Wood and Connaught Cemetery*
12 *The Memorial to the Missing, Thiepval*
13 *Authuille Village and Authuille Wood*
14 *Blighty Valley Cemetery*
15 *Ovillers Military Cemetery*
a *Mash Valley*
B *La Boisselle Village*
c *Sausage Valley*
16 *'Y'-sap Mine Crater*
17 *Tyneside Memorial Seat*
18 *Lochnagar Mine Crater (the 'Great Mine')*
19 *German Cemetery, Fricourt*
20 *Fricourt New British Cemetery*
21 *Triple Tambour Mine Craters*
22 *Fricourt British Cemetery, Bray Road*
23 *Dartmoor Cemetery, Becordel*
24 *Point 110 Old and New Cemeteries*
25 *Devonshire Cemetery and Mansell Copse*
26 *Gordon Cemetery*
27 *Carnoy Military Cemetery*
28 *Kasino Point Mine Crater*
29 *Peronne Road Cemetery, Maricourt*
30 *Flatiron Copse Cemetery*
31 *Bernafay Wood Cemetery*
32 *18th Division Memorial, Trones Wood*
33 *Guillemont Road Cemetery*
34 *Delville Wood Cem./South African Mem'l.*
35 *New Zealand Memorial*
36 *47th London Division Memorial, High Wood*
37 *London Cemetery and Extension, High Wood*
38 *Pozieres British Cemetery and Memorial to the Missing on the Somme of 1918*
39 *The Tank Corps Memorial, Pozieres*
40 *Australian Division Memorial, Pozieres*
41 *Canadian Memorial, Courcelette*
42 *The Butte de Warlencourt*
43 *Newfoundland Memorial, Gueudecourt*

Warning! *The intense artillery bombardment of the Somme area has led to many shells still being unearthed today. Grenades, bullets and other debris are also found. But,* BE WARNED, *a lot of this material is live and very dangerous because explosives become more unstable with age.* SO DO NOT TOUCH ANY OF THESE ITEMS AT ANY TIME!

The Town of Albert:-

Before 1914: Albert, previously known as Ancre after the river that flows through it, was a small, undistinguished town with narrow cobbled streets, typical of northern France. It lay about 22 km north-east of Amiens, the regional centre of the Somme department. Although set amidst rich farmland, Albert was an industrial town, having several iron foundries. The only really notable feature of the town was the impressive basilica. As can be seen in the pre-war photograph opposite, the tower was topped by a statue of the Virgin Mary holding up the infant Jesus. The gilded statue was known as the 'Golden Virgin'.

(photo: Lelong; 21 Rue St Martin, Amiens.)

During the war; 1914 - early 1918: *When the Germans marched into France in 1914, Albert was one of the places where the French army managed to halt their progress. Albert was, in fact, briefly occupied by the Germans in late September 1914, but they were driven out by the French, who held the whole of the Somme sector at that time. It was then that the opposing sets of front line trenches were set up, about 3 km east of the town. The French held Albert and the lower ground to the west of the line, while the Germans held the higher ground of the Pozieres Ridge to the east (map p4 and 6). From then on Albert was at the centre of the subsequent Somme battles. First French, and then British troops sheltered in its cellars or passed through the town on their way up to the front line. As a consequence, Albert was very heavily shelled by the Germans, the Golden Virgin providing a marker for them to aim at. On January 15th 1915 the Golden Virgin was nearly toppled when the dome of the tower was hit by a shell. The photograph opposite, taken in September 1916, shows that the Virgin ended up at a precarious angle. She became the 'Leaning Virgin', and a legend grew that until she fell the war would not finish.* (IWM Q 855)

In 1918: *In their Spring Offensive of 1918 the Germans not only recaptured all of their previously held territory on the Somme, but they moved even further westwards, taking Albert on March 26th 1918, and then threatening to take Amiens (see p 4 and 5, and p 37). The town of Albert was now in German hands, and the British and French had fallen back to stand resolutely before Amiens, determined not to allow the Germans to take it and break through to the coast.*

When the British had held Albert they had used the basilica tower as an artillery observation post, the extra height allowing them to see the effect their shelling was having on the German positions on the Pozieres Ridge. When, in 1918, the Germans held Albert the British were determined that they should not use the tower for the same purpose. So, on April 16th 1918, it was British shells that brought the basilica tower crashing down, and with it the 'Leaning Virgin'. The photograph above shows the result of the British shelling. It was taken on August 22nd 1918, the day that the British recaptured Albert in their final offensive against the Germans which eventually led to the end of the war in November 1918 (see p 38). So, the legend about the 'Leaning Virgin' turned out to have an element of truth in it because the war ended within a few months of her fall. But, sadly, by that time hundreds of thousands of men had died and many villages and towns were, like Albert, totally destroyed. (IWM Q 11201)

After the war: Today, a plaque on the Town Hall wall in Albert says of the town in 1918 that: *"Nothing remained but name, glory and the ruins".* But very soon after the war work was begun to rebuild Albert. Special care was taken to reconstruct the basilica as it was before. As the modern photograph opposite shows, the result of this effort is that once again Albert is overlooked by a magnificent Golden Virgin holding up the infant Christ. This new statue, visible from many places on the old Somme battlefield - just as the original was - seems to symbolize people's efforts to make up for the mistakes of the past.

Albert makes an excellent centre from which to visit the Somme battlefields today, but the town itself should not be overlooked. A number of the shops sell postcard photographs depicting the original town and its destruction during the war. A look around you provides living proof of its reconstruction. This same pattern is repeated in the countryside to the east of the town. The villages that were destroyed during the battles of the Somme have all been rebuilt, and the shell-torn land has been returned to peaceful farmland.

Holding the Somme line 1915-16; an individual case:-

The story of Bill Beckington:

The first intimation of a casualty among the 7th West Kents has been received this week, as on Wednesday morning Mr. and Mrs. Beckington, of 26, Camden-grove, Chislehurst, had the distressing tidings that their son, Private William Leslie Beckington, had been killed in action a week previously. They were not unprepared for the news, as on Tuesday the parents of another Chislehurst soldier had had it conveyed to them in a letter from their son. No intimation has been received from the War Office, but on Wednesday morning Mr. and Mrs. Beckington received the following letter, which, although the news which it contains was so sad, no parent could read without a feeling of gratification:—

Dear Mrs. Beckington,—I am very sorry to have to tell you that your son was killed while in a working party on Wednesday, August 24th. He was in the front line trench within twenty yards of the enemy. I had known him for over a year, as he was in my platoon, and I was very fond of him. Although my youngest man, he had always stuck the marches, however long, and never complained, being a great favourite. He was shot through the head and died immediately, being buried at 7 o'clock in the evening. Many of his friends, both officers and men, attended. A simple cross now marks the spot where one of England's bravest and happiest soldiers was buried. The one great consolation is that he died fighting for his country in the front line. —Hoping that pride will help you to bear the sorrow, I remain, yours sincerely, J. B. Matthews, Lieutenant.

Mr. and Mrs. Beckington have indeed lost a brave son, and sympathy will go out to them in the death of their only boy. Of a bright disposition, and possessed of that spice of daring natural to a true-hearted English lad, Private Beckington was well-liked by all who knew him. Coming of a patriotic family—his father has been an orderly at the Red Cross Hospital since it was opened, and his mother has also done much useful voluntary help there—he was quick to respond to his country's call, and although only 17 on the 11th of August, he joined the West Kents on September 9th of last year. With a number of other Chislehurst lads he took part in the happy farewell gathering in St. Mary's Hall on July 9th, and evidently soon after left for the Front. He spent his eighteenth birthday in the trenches, and a few hours before he met his death he wrote home saying that he was perfectly happy.

A: *Bill, front row, second right, at Chislehurst in 1914.*

B: *Frank Bastable, standing, right, recalls Bill's death:*

We hadn't been in the line long, first time up on our own really - August 1915 it was. Bill Beckington and me, a pal of mine from Chislehurst, we were told to go up and repair a trench. A shell had made a gap in the front of this trench, all blown down it was. Well, we got there and we got some sandbags. He said "I'll go up and you fill the bags and hand them up to me". But as soon as he went up there was a sound, and something went past. A sniper!. I was just going to say "Look out Bill, I think he's got you spotted", when there was another shot and Bill was hit in the head. I can still see it now, bits of his brains on my tunic there was - like fishes roe. He couldn't have known what hit him. He was the first chap to get it in our Company. They should have told us to keep down - we were new, we didn't know. We carried him back, not far, and I remember we buried him in the evening. I was lucky, if I'd gone up and he'd filled the sandbags, it would have been me that got hit. That's the sort of thing you think about afterwards really. Poor Bill - they should have told us.

C: *Bill's grave in Point 110 Old Cemetery just to the south of Fricourt.* *(see 24 on the map on p6)*

D: *An article in the* Chislehurst and District Times *for Sept. 3rd 1915 concerning Bill's death. (By permission of the British Library: Newspaper Library, London)*

Frank Bastable, *now 86, told me Bill Beckington's story. They had both joined the army at Chislehurst, Kent in September 1914, one month after war broke out. They were both allotted to 'C' Company of the 7th Battalion Royal West Kent Regiment. Frank was the son of a fishmonger in Chislehurst, and like many other lads, at 18 was looking for a more exciting life. This was the period when no one really foresaw the horror of the war, and many rushed to become a part of it for fear it would be 'all over by Christmas'. After training in England, the 7th West Kents landed in France in July 1915, and from then until 1916 was involved in 'holding the Somme line' - mainly between Becourt and Carnoy. The Somme was a 'quiet' sector of the Western Front at that time. However, even in 'quiet' times many men were killed. Shelling, machine-guns and snipers all took their toll each day. And so it was that the death of Bill Beckington occurred in August 1915 (but was it on the 24th or the 25th?). The field, oral, and documentary evidence (see opposite and the Battalion War Diary extract on p 1) help us piece the sad story together.*

Frank gets ten days 'Number One Field Punishment': The usual pattern was for the soldiers to spend about ten days up at the front line trenches, and then ten days back in the billets for a rest, though this period always included training and other duties that were far from restful. The villages just behind the front line on the Somme had been taken over as billets for the troops. Frank Bastable's Battalion, the 7th West Kents, were billeted in Dernancourt, about 6 km behind the front line (see map p6), for much of the time from August 1915 to March 1916. During the winter of 1915-16 Frank experienced a particularly uncomfortable ten days while in billets:

> We'd just come out of the trenches. The sergeant must have forgotten to tell us to unload, and as I was Mess Orderly next day I didn't have time to clean my rifle. So, when I went on parade next morning my rifle was still loaded, though I didn't remember it was of course! When I opened and closed the bolt for inspection, I accidentally let off a round. I had to go before the C.O., and I got ten days Number One Field Punishment. They brought up these wagons, I thought I had to clean them - really muddy they were, but instead they strapped me up to one of the wheels, by my ankles and my wrists. Two hours a day I had of that, one in the morning and one in the afternoon. The worst thing was the cold, it was winter, and there were some shells coming over - but the cold was the worst thing. Thankfully, they let me run round a bit in between to get warmed up. I didn't like it much I can tell you, you looked such a fool.

Summer 1916 soon arrived and the defensive task gave way to the Allied Offensive in July, but Bill Beckington had already died, 'holding the Somme line'.

'First Somme'; Preliminary Bombardment, June 1916:-

British 9·2″ gun *in use on July 1st 1916, at the conclusion of the preliminary bombardment of the German positions on the Somme. The bombardment went on for a week prior to the attack itself, with a total of 1500 guns firing more than 1¾ million rounds.* (IWM Q 46)

The plan: The Allied Army Commanders knew that the German defences on the Somme were very strong indeed. The Germans had built several defence lines, each one comprising a number of trench lines, barbed wire and machine-gun posts. They had also fortified the villages in their lines (see maps on pages 4 and 6). They also had heavy artillery. The Allies thus realized that any attack would have to be preceded by a heavy, accurate and lengthy bombardment if the advancing soldiers were to stand any chance at all. It was planned to explode some mines under the German front line just prior to the attack itself, but there were only to be a few of these (see pages 14,22 and 24), and so most effort had to be put into destroying the Germans' defences over the whole of the 20 km Somme front. The aim was to obliterate the German trenches, and destroy the machine-gun posts and the fortified villages. In so doing the German soldiers would be killed, captured or forced to retreat. It was also planned to destroy or cut the German barbed wire defences. By careful ground and aerial spotting it was intended that the German artillery batteries would be located and put out of action by the bombardment so that they could not shell the advancing Allied troops on the day of the attack. The bombardment thus began on June 24th 1916.

It was originally intended that the bombardment should last for five days, with the attack planned for June 29th ('Z' day). This plan was later changed, with the bombardment extended by two days ('Y1' and 'Y2' days) which resulted in the attack taking place on July 1st 1916. During the first two days it was intended to concentrate on cutting the German wire by shelling, and also to spot and knock out the German artillery. In the remaining three days (before the original plan was changed; see opposite), wire-cutting and counter-artillery battery work was to continue, and the destruction of the German trenches, fortified villages, and machine-gun posts was also to take place. It was assumed that such a bombardment would lead to an unopposed Allied attack (see section below).

1: The theory:-

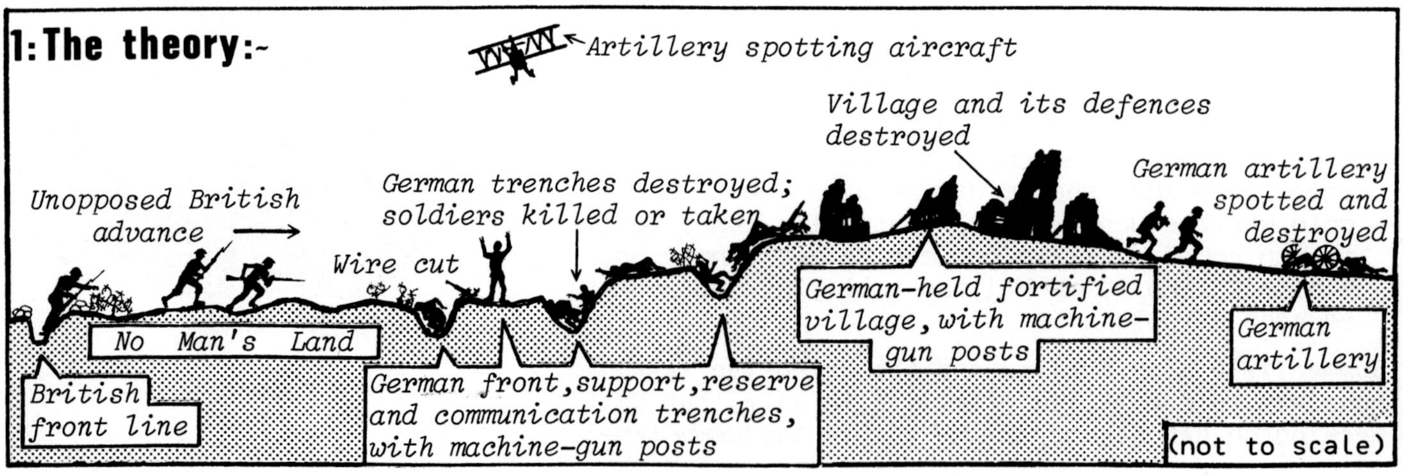

Men of the 1st Lancashire Fusiliers

fixing bayonets prior to their attack on Beaumont Hamel on July 1st 1916 (see p14). Men such as these, all along the Somme front that morning, relied upon the heavy bombardment having done what it was meant to do; unfortunately, in most sectors it had not. (IWM Q 744)

What actually happened: Attempts at wire-cutting went on throughout the first three days of the bombardment, but counter-battery work was dependent upon good weather to allow aerial spotting. The weather was very variable at first, but on days 4 and 5 mist and low cloud prevented any chance of such work taking place. Night raids into the German lines produced conflicting reports, some saying the German trenches were destroyed and empty while others that they were not; some said the wire was cut, others not. The large number of 'dud' shells, with wrong or faulty fuses, made wire-cutting particularly difficult, and insufficient guns and ammunition, along with poor observation conditions, all contributed to a less than satisfactory result. It was thus decided to extend the bombardment by two days, but this helped little as it turned out, only causing the troops to be held in damp trenches for two days waiting to go 'over the top'. The best that could be reported in most sectors was that the German wire was 'passable' in places.

Although some of the German trenches and the villages they held were badly damaged, the German soldiers themselves had mostly survived. They did so by sheltering in deep dug-outs which they had constructed beneath the trenches and the ruins of the villages. As soon as the bombardment ceased, clear indication that an attack was about to begin, the German soldiers emerged. The British also used a 'creeping barrage' of shells on July 1st, starting on the German front line and 'lifting' from there at 7.30 a.m., moving on in steps (hence 'creeping') over the back lines to a pre-arranged, unchangeable time-table, according to the rate at which the infantry was expected to advance. However, as the barrage had lifted from their front line at 7.30 a.m., there were no shells to hinder the Germans as they emerged from their dug-outs and set up their machine-guns. Too few guns and too big an area to shell led to the preliminary bombardment being largely ineffective. Poor communications led to the creeping barrage being mostly wasted effort. But whatever the reason, the advancing British troops were killed by German machine-gun bullets and shells on July 1st that they had been led to believe would no longer exist.

2:The reality:-

'First Somme'; Hawthorn Ridge/Beaumont Hamel, July 1st 1916:-

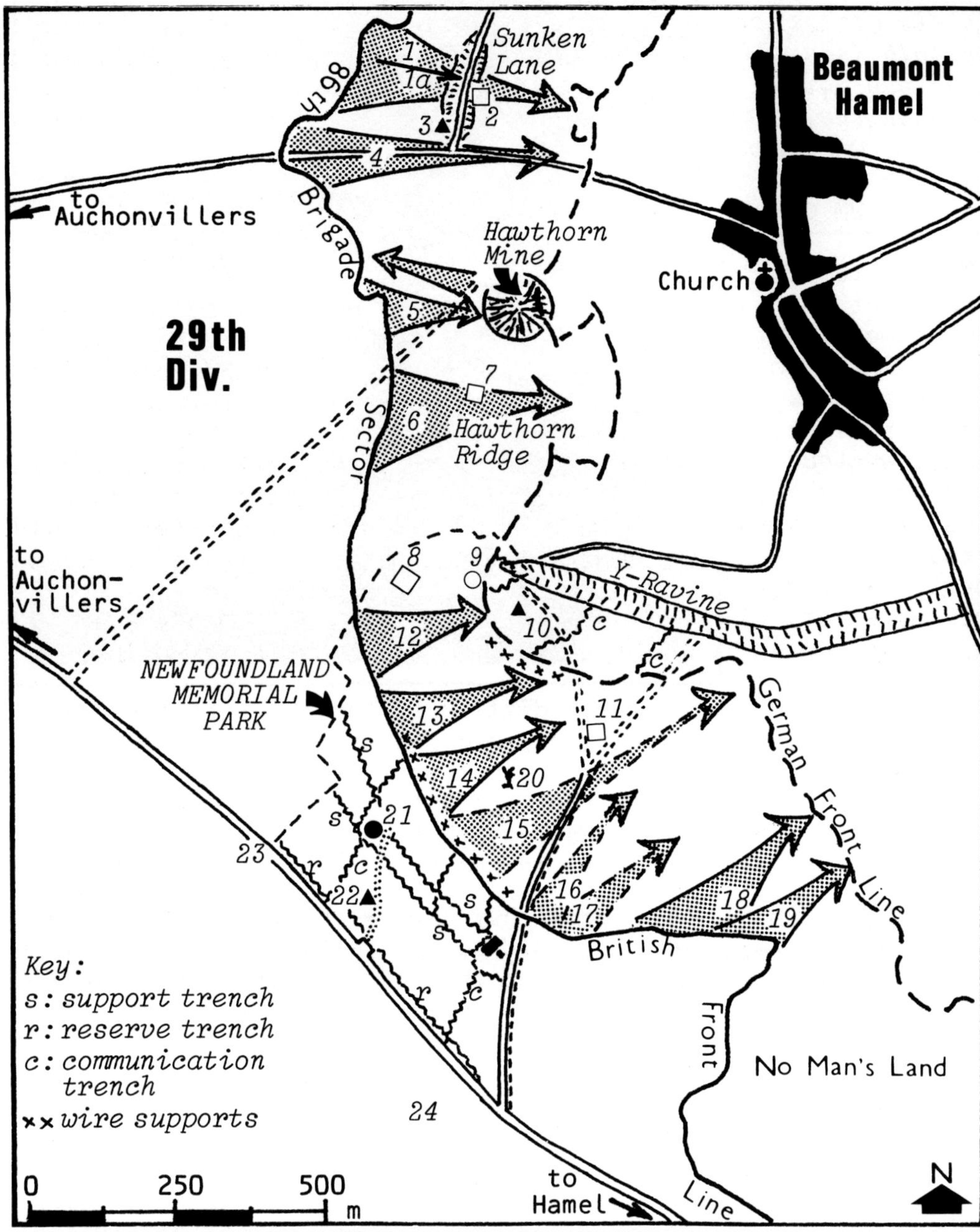

29th DIV. ATTACK ON BEAUMONT HAMEL, July 1st 1916

- ——— *British Front Line*
- — — *German Front Line*
- 1 *1st Lancs. Fusiliers*
- 1a *Shallow tunnels to the Sunken Lane*
- 4 *16th Middlesex Regt.*
- 5 *2nd Royal Fusiliers (part) attack crater*
- 6 *2nd Royal Fusiliers/ 1st R.Dublin Fusil.*
- 12/14 *2nd S.Wales Border*
- 13 *1st Border Regiment*
- 15 *1st Newfoundland Regt*
- 16/19 *1st King's Own Scottish Borderers*
- 17 *1st Essex Regiment*
- 18 *1st R.Innisk'ng.Fusil*
- 23 *1st Newfoundland, and*
- 24 *1st Essex held in reserve until c 8.45 a.m.*
- 2 *Beaumont Hamel Cem.*
- 3 *8th Argyle and Sutherland Highlanders Mem. to 51st Div. attack on Nov.13th 1916*
- 7 *Hawthorn Ridge Cem. 1*
- 8 *Hawthorn Ridge Cem. 2*
- 9 *Hunter's Cemetery*
- 10 *51st Div.Mem.to attack on Nov.13th 1916*
- 11 *'Y'-Ravine Cemetery*
- 20 *The 'Danger Tree'*
- 21 *The Newfoundland Caribou Memorial*
- 22 *29th Div.Memorial to July 1st 1916 attack*

The Hawthorn mine *exploding beneath the German front line on Hawthorn Ridge at 7.20 a.m. on July 1st 1916, at the beginning of the 29th Division attack on Beaumont Hamel.* (IWM Q 754)

The bombardment of the German positions continued in the early hours of July 1st 1916, but then, at around 7.30 a.m., the barrage lifted and the infantry attack began. It was along a 40 km front, the northern sector British, the southern French. The main part of this book describes some of the events of the 'First Battle of the Somme' by following the British sector from north to south, starting at Beaumont Hamel (Serre and Gommecourt have been omitted).

Hawthorn Ridge: 86th Brigade of the 29th Div. were set the task of attacking Beaumont Hamel across the Hawthorn Ridge(see map opposite). However, despite the exploding of a mine beneath the German lines ten minutes before the main attack, and the digging of tunnels to the Sunken Lane to give the 1st Lancashire Fusiliers a forward starting position at 7.30 a.m. , the attack of the 86th was doomed to failure. An extract from the War Diary of the 1st Lancashire Fusiliers for July 1st 1916 gives some indication of what happened on that day on Hawthorn Ridge:

> The Battalion was badly cut up by the enemy's M.G. (machine-gun) fire. Suffering 508 casualties and 21 officer casualties. ..... The Battalion fought nobly but had no chance against enemy's M.G. fire. *(PRO WO 95/2300)*

There were several reasons for this state of affairs. The preliminary bombardment had led the Germans to expect an attack, and the exploding of some mines along the British front near 7.30 a.m. on the 1st announced that it was about to begin. On Hawthorn Ridge it had been decided to blow the mine ten minutes before the main attack, not two minutes as with the other mines, to allow the 2nd Royal Fusiliers time to occupy the mine crater and use it as a forward attacking position. Unfortunately, to allow this the bombardment also had to be lifted at 7.20 a.m. This gave the Germans plenty of time, unmolested by shelling, to emerge from their dug-outs (see p 13) and set up their machine guns ready for the British soldiers to advance. Also, as the bombardment had failed to knock out the German artillery, a barrage of German shells began to fall on the soldiers as soon as the attack began. Finally, the very few who made it across No Man's Land found that the German wire was largely un-cut and were shot, caught upon its barbs.

The attack by the 1st Lancashire Fusiliers (see 1/1a on map) failed only a few yards beyond the Sunken Lane. Half the battalion became casualties (see War Diary above. A full battalion is about 1100 men). Only a few men made it to the small bank beyond the Lane, where some still lie today in the small Beaumont Hamel Cemetery (see 2 on map). The 2nd Royal Fusiliers also suffered badly from the German machine-gun fire. Those detailed to occupy the mine crater found, as many had feared, that the Germans quickly occupied part of the crater and were using it as an extra defensive position. By noon the whole crater had to be given up to the Germans. To complete the sad story, the 16th Middlesex and 1st Royal Dublin Fusiliers were sent in at 8.00 a.m. despite the failure of the first attack. Men of these battalions therefore also lie in the Hawthorn Cemeteries (see 7 & 8). So, at the end of the day, no ground had been won, but the attack had cost the 86th Bde. nearly 2000 casualties, including over 600 dead.

It was not until Nov.13th 1916 that Hawthorn Ridge and Beaumont Hamel were taken by the 51st (Scottish) Division. Evidence of this can also be seen in the cemeteries as well as in the 8th Argyle and Sutherland Highlanders monument at 3 on the map opposite. So it had taken over three months to capture an objective originally planned to take hours.

Section:

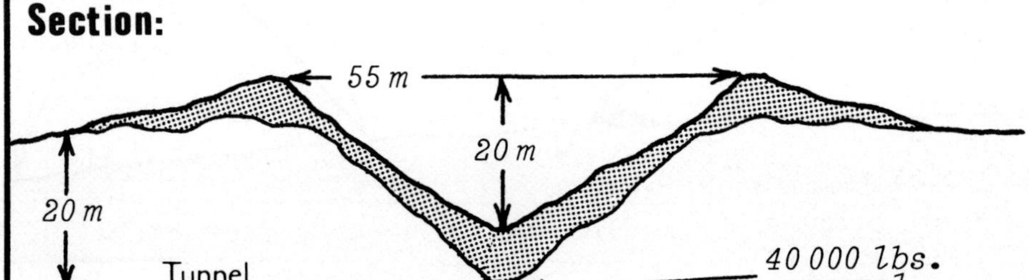

Hawthorn mine crater *is an impressive piece of field evidence of the events which took place on Hawthorn Ridge on July 1st 1916. But even the explosion of this mine did not help the 86th Bde. to break through to Beaumont Hamel. The explosion of a second mine here on Nov.13th 1916, however, did help the 51st Div.to take the village very near the end of the 'First Battle of the Somme'. Because infill has only been slight, the crater has kept its original profile well.*

The Newfoundland Memorial Park, Beaumont Hamel:-

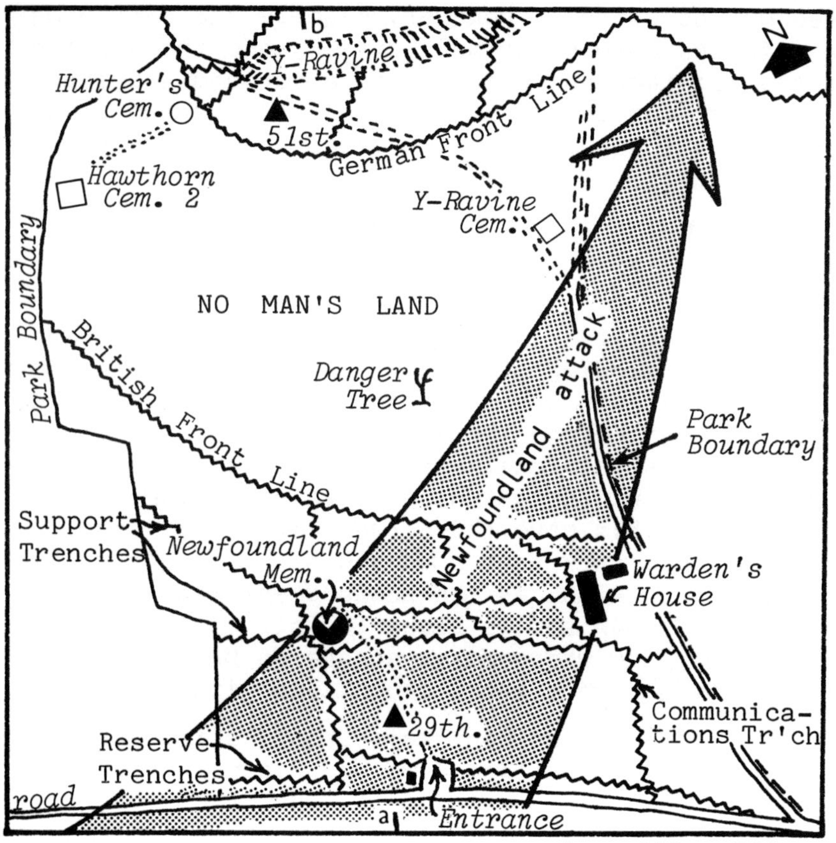

1: Map

The Park *has preserved within it both the British and the German lines of 1916, with No Man's Land in between. There are also monuments to the 29th and 51st Divs. and three cemeteries (see map opposite). The Park is here because the Newfoundland Government bought the land to preserve it as a memorial to the men of the 1st Newfoundland Regt. who fought and died here on July 1st 1916 in the 29th Div. attack on Beaumont Hamel (see map p14 and the account of their action on pp 18-19).*

It is possible to walk this ground today and imagine the events of July 1st 1916. The British trenches, the wire supports, No Man's Land - with the preserved 'Danger Tree' around which many men died that day - all evoke a strong feeling of the past. Looking back from the German lines, it is easy to see that the advancing British soldiers stood little chance against the German machine-guns.

2: Section

Newfoundland Caribou Memorial

British Front Line

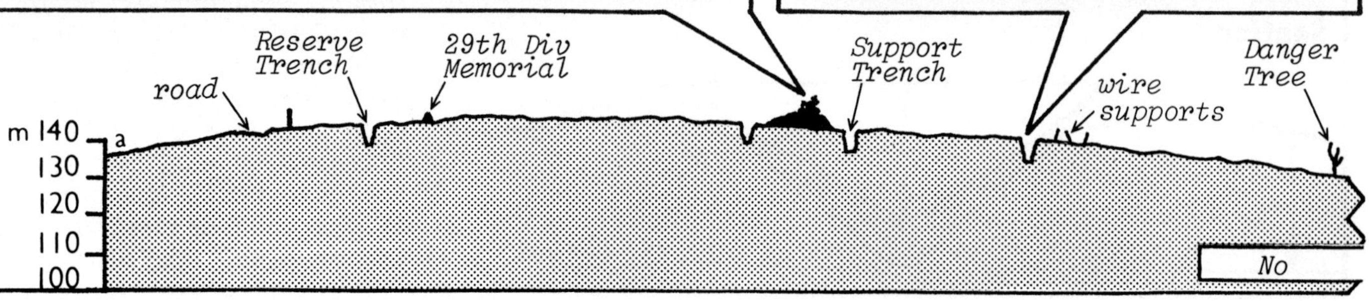

29th Div. attack, July 1st: The attack just to the south of Beaumont Hamel was led by the 87th Bde. of 29th Div. The 2nd South Wales Borderers and 1st Royal Inniskilling Fusiliers went 'over the top' first, closely followed in support by the 1st King's Own Scottish Borderers and the 1st Border Regt. (see map p14). They were to storm the German front line and 'Y'-Ravine, take the first objective, Beaumont Hamel, and then move on to the second objective, the German intermediate line 1 km east of the village. The reserves, 88th Bde., including the Newfoundlanders, were then to move up and take the third objective, the German Second Line about 4 km east of the village. A 'creeping barrage' was arranged to help this advance, with artillery 'lifts' at pre-determined, unchangeable times, viz. off the German front line at 'zero' (7.30 a.m.), off the second objective 40 minutes later, and off the third objective after 3½ Hrs by which time the infantry were planned to have reached the German Second Line of defences east of Beaumont Hamel.

The German soldiers had sheltered from the British preliminary bombardment in dug-outs in 'Y'-Ravine; these being connected to their front line trenches. As the British 'creeping' artillery barrage lifted from here at 'zero', the Germans could emerge and set up their machine-guns unmolested (a common event that day). The German wire was also uncut, though the convexity of slope (see section below) hid this fact. Few of the 1st R. Inniskillings reached the German wire, and even fewer went beyond it. In front of 'Y'-Ravine, the 2nd South Wales Borderers never even got close to the German wire, being practically all mown down by three German heavy machine-guns, not even visible to them beyond the slope in front of the German line, by 7.35 a.m. A German artillery barrage of the British front, support and reserve trenches killed many of the men of the support battalions before they even reached their own front line. Those that did were easily cut down by the German machine-gunners as they were forced to bunch-up when passing through the too narrow, and too few, lanes cut in our wire for the advancing soldiers. Without the support of an artillery barrage, which had now moved on beyond recall, the 87th Bde. advance stood no chance of success, and it 'melted away' soon after 8.00 a.m. But the tragedy was not over; another act, involving the Newfoundlanders, was beginning.

German Front Line

'Y'-Ravine

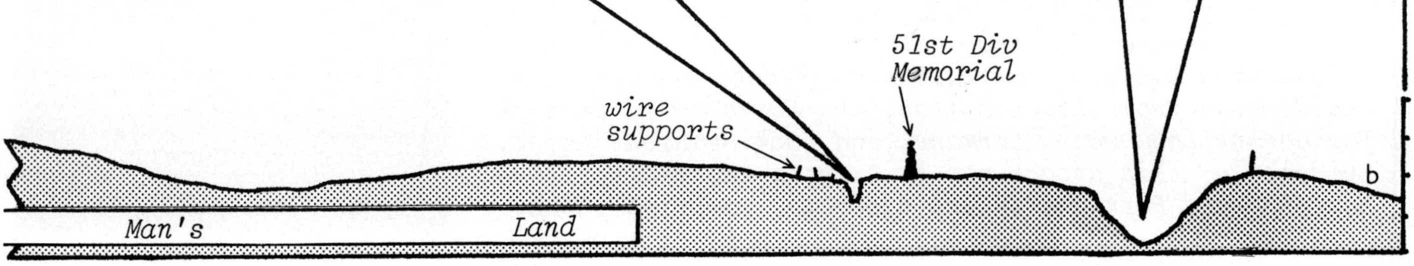

The Newfoundland attack, July 1st: Somehow, reports suggesting that the 87th Bde. attack had been successful in certain respects reached 29th Div.H.Q. Therefore, at 8.45 a.m., two of the reserve battalions of 88th Bde., the 1st Newfoundland and the 1st Essex Regt., were ordered forward. As the entry for July 1st 1916 in the Newfoundland Regiment War Diary says (see opposite), they were ordered to "occupy enemy's first trench". The Diary helps unfold the rest of the sad story of the Newfoundlander's attack. Before they advanced at 9.15 a.m. their C.O. tried to find out what the situation actually was that he was to send his men into. He got no clear answer, only that he could go forward independently of the 1st Essex Regiment.

The Newfoundlanders and the 1st Essex were assembled in the reserve trench along the Hamel-Auchonvillers road (preserved today just inside the entrance to the Newfoundland Park, see map p16). The 1st Essex attack was in fact delayed for an hour, the time it took them to get to their own front line through communication trenches clogged with the dead and wounded of 87th Bde. To avoid a similar hold-up, the Newfoundlanders moved forward "direct over the open" from the reserve trench, the lone battalion exposed to German machine-gun fire and shelling for about 250 m before even reaching their own front lines (see map and section p16). The Diary indicates that they advanced 'by the book', i.e. with the men properly spaced according to the formation prescribed for assaulting infantry, and all at walking pace!. Many of the men were thus cut down before they even reached their own wire and, when the survivors did so, the disaster was completed. The Newfoundlanders had to 'bunch-up' in order to pass through the all too few lanes cut in their own wire and here, as their War Diary graphically describes, they were "mown down in heaps". Only a few made it down the slope into No Man's Land, past the 'Danger Tree' and on to the German lines, where they too were shot. With a total of about 700 casualties, including over 230 dead, out of 800 who had gone into action, the 1st Newfoundland Regiment had been virtually annihilated - for no gain whatsoever.

Shortly after 10.00 a.m. the attack was halted and, despite attempts to mount a second attack later in the day, on the evening of July 1st Beaumont Hamel was still in German hands. The only thing that had changed was that over 1800 men of 29th Div. were dead or missing, and over 3000 wounded. However, because the Newfoundlanders suffered most casualties on that fateful day, it is fitting that part of the battlefield where the 29th Div. fought should be preserved in their honour, and that their emblem, the caribou, should stand proudly above it. To visit Newfoundland Park is to walk through history.

51st Div. attack, Nov. 13th 1916: *Beaumont Hamel remained in German hands to very near the end of 'First Somme'. On Nov. 13th 1916, 51st (Scottish) Div. attacked along the old 29th Div. front, but their bombardment and barrage was more effective. Starting at 5.45 a.m., when a second mine was blown at Hawthorn - effectively removing the Germans from that position, the Scots moved through fog against now weary Germans, and took Beaumont Hamel. Evidence of this attack can be seen in the cemeteries in Newfoundland Park and in the 51st Div. memorial there.*

General attack all along the line

6.00–07.30 Intense bombardment

7.30. 86th & 87th Brigades attacked 1st system of enemy trenches. 88th Bde, under prearranged orders were to move forward at 0840 to attack 3rd line system of trenches. About 0820 received orders not to move until further orders. Presumably the first attack not having been successful.

08.45. Received orders on telephone to move forward in conjunction with Essex Regt. and occupy enemy's first trench – our objective being point (89) to just north of point (60). and work forward to Station Road clearing the enemy trenches – and move as soon as possible. Asked Brigade if enemies 1st trench has been taken and received reply to the effect that the situation was not cleared up. Asked Brigade if we were to move off to attack independently of Essex Regt. and received reply in affirmative.

09.15. Reported to Brigade that Newfoundland Regt. was moving off. It was subsequently found that the Essex Regt. did not attack until 0955 i.e. after our attack had failed. The Regiment moved off in previously arranged formation i.e. A & B Companies (A on left) in 1st line in lines of platoons in file or single file at 40 paces interval and 25 paces between sections – followed by C & D Coys (C on left) in similar formation at 100 yards distance. C Coy. had been specially detailed as consolidating company and therefore carried additional equipment. The advance was made direct over the open from the rear trenches known as St John's Road and Clonmel Avenue. As soon as the signal for advance was given the regiment left the trenches and moved steadily forward machine gun fire from our right front was at once opened on us and then artillery fire also. The distance to our objective varied from 650 to 900 yards. The enemy's fire was effective from the outset but the heaviest casualties occurred on passing through the gaps in our front wire where the men were mown down in heaps. Many more gaps in the wire were required than had been cut. In spite of losses the survivors steadily advanced until close to the enemies wire by which time very few remained. A few men are believed to have actually succeeded in throwing bombs into the enemy's trench.

July 1st 1916; a page from the War Diary of the 1st Newfoundland Regiment *provides an important and evocative form of documentary evidence that helps us discover what happened to the Newfoundlanders on that fateful day. The Public Record Office at Kew in London holds the originals of War Diaries for all the battalions involved in the First World War. They detail the times, places and events with an impression of immediacy resulting from the fact that they were written on the field of battle. They provide an excellent complement to photographic, oral, and field evidence.*

(By kind permission of the Controller of H.M.S.O.; Public Record Office, London; document reference: WO 95/2308)

Thiepval and the Schwaben Redoubt, July 1st 1916:-

The view from Connaught Cemetery, site of the British front line at 7.30 a.m. on July 1st 1916. The Ulstermen of 36th Division advanced up this slope towards the German front line, where Mill Road Cemetery is today, and on to the Schwaben Redoubt beyond.

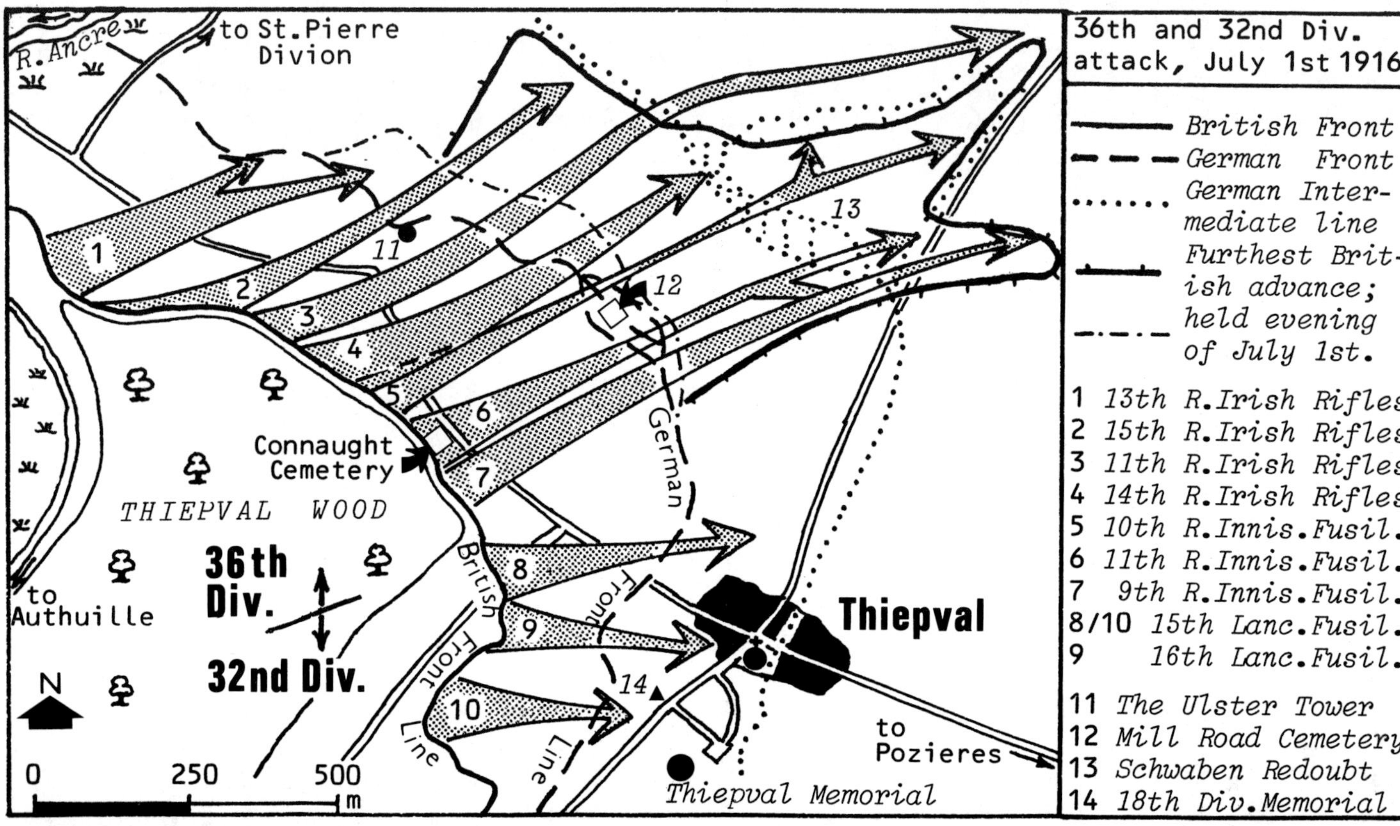

The 36th (Ulster) Division sector of the Somme front on July 1st lay astride the marshy valley of the River Ancre. Their left flank was on the higher ground north of the river (adjoining 29th Div.) where they attempted, unsuccessfully, to move up the valley towards Grandcourt (maps p4 & 6). Their right flank (map above) was on high ground south of the river, the northern end of Pozieres Ridge. Their task was to cross the Ridge and take the German Second Line near Grandcourt. In their path lay not only the German front line but, just beyond it, the intermediate line within which was the Schwaben Redoubt. The Germans had several such strong-points along the Somme front, between their fortified villages. They comprised a system of trenches capable of being defended from all directions, and beneath them there were large dug-outs where the German soldiers were able to shelter from the British heavy bombardment and attack barrage.

Looking north *from the 18th Div.Memorial towards the slope up which the Ulstermen advanced on July 1st.* **TW:** *Thiepval Wood;* **CC:** *Connaught Cem.(old British front line);* **UT:** *Ulster Tower(36th Div.Mem'l);* **MRC:** *Mill Road Cemetery(old German front line);* **SR:** *site of the Schwaben Redoubt(German Int.line).*

Looking south *from Mill Road Cemetery towards the village of Thiepval and the Memorial to the Missing, which is on the site of the old Thiepval Chateau. The village is smaller today than in 1914.*

On the Ulstermen's right lay the left flank of the 32nd Div. Their task was to take the 'fortress' village of Thiepval. Although the British bombardment had reduced the village and the Chateau to rubble, the cellars were intact and they made excellent shelters and machine-gun nests. The whole of the western side of the village, including the Chateau site, had been turned by the Germans into a chain of very strong machine-gun posts.

On July 1st, following a very effective preliminary bombardment(unusually so for this part of the front), the Ulstermen quickly took the German front line, and moved to the crest so rapidly that the Germans had no time to come up from their dug-outs in the Schwaben Redoubt, which was thus also taken. So successful was the advance that by 10.00 a.m. some Royal Irish Rifles had reached the German Second Line south of Grandcourt where, unfortunately, they came under their own barrage, not due to lift from there until 10.10 a.m. However, this successful penetration of the German lines had to be largely given up before nightfall because it was not matched by the attacks up the Ancre valley to the north or on Thiepval to the south. The Lancashire and Northumberland Fusiliers, on the left of the 32nd Div., were cut down by the German machine-gunners in Thiepval, and attempts to take the village had been abandoned. The Ulstermen were thus exposed in a narrow salient, open to attack from three sides, and were running out of ammunition and supplies. A full German counter attack at 10.00 p.m. finally forced them to withdraw, giving up virtually all their gains, including the Schwaben Redoubt. The village of Thiepval was not to fall to the British until late September, and the Schwaben Redoubt remained in German hands until mid-October 1916 (see brief details below).

Frank Bastable, *of the 7th West Kents (see p10), moved towards Thiepval on Sept.28th 1916 as part of the 55th Bde. of 18th Div. The 53rd & 54th Bdes. of that Div. had already helped take Thiepval on the 27th, but Schwaben Redoubt was yet to be won. The 55th,including Frank, went up to help:*

> I'd just got back from being wounded(see p31). Just getting up to Thiepval was difficult. The shelling was so bad, I thought I'd had it that time. I dived under a farm cart by the road, it made me feel better, but I don't suppose it would have helped much against a direct hit!.

Early on the 29th, the 7th West Kents took over the line in front of the Schwaben and fought hard all that day and into the night. Headstones like that opposite, in Mill Road Cem., and the 18th Div.Memorial(14 on map) are evidence of their attacks. The Schwaben finally fell to 39th Div. on Oct. 14th.

La Boisselle and Ovillers, July 1st 1916:-

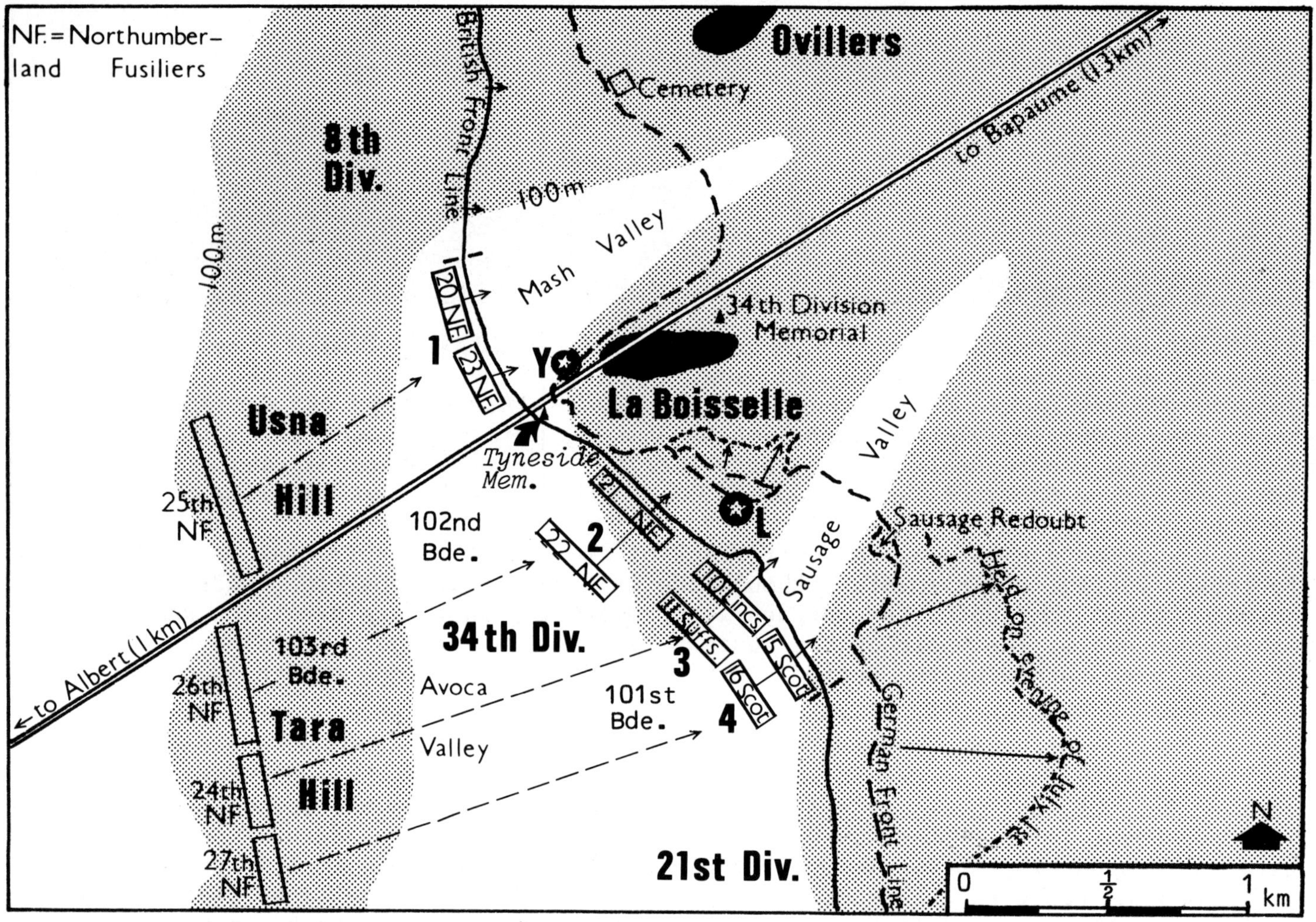

The Lochnagar Mine (**L** on map), blown at 7.28 a.m. on July 1st as part of 34th Div's. attack, made a huge crater that has been preserved for us to see today. Flying above the lines that morning, 2nd Lt. C.A.Lewis, R.F.C., saw the mine explode:

> The whole earth heaved and flared, a tremendous and magnificent column rose up into the sky. There was an ear-splitting roar, drowning all the guns, flinging the machine sideways in the repercussing air. The earth column rose higher and higher to almost 4,000 feet.

From *Sagittarius Rising*: C.A.Lewis

Section:

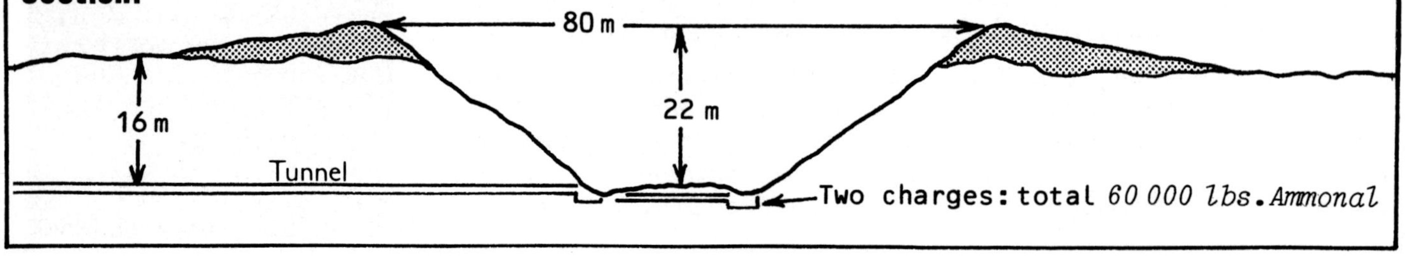

Men of 103rd (Tyneside Irish) Brigade advancing on La Boisselle, *July 1st 1916. The 103rd began their advance at the same time, 7.30 a.m., as the 101st and the 102nd Bdes. in the all-out effort to break through at La Boisselle, but from the 'Tara-Usna Line' on a low ridge about 1½ km behind the British front line. During this long advance many of the men were mown down by German machine-gunners in La Boisselle as the open Avoca Valley provided no cover for them. The 103rd and 102nd (Tyneside Scottish) Bdes. are commemorated in a memorial seat near La Boisselle.* (IWM Q 53)

The 34th (& 8th) Div. attack astride the Pozieres/Bapaume Road was crucial in the overall plan to break through to Bapaume. Consequently, all battalions of 34th and 8th Divs. were ordered to advance at 7.30 a.m. on July 1st. The 34th launched a four-pronged attack on La Boisselle and Sausage Valley, each with two leading battalions and one of 103rd Bde. starting from the Tara-Usna Line. 8th Div. attacked Ovillers and Mash Valley, helped there by the 102nd Bde. The German trenches and the fortified villages of La-Boisselle and Ovillers were to be destroyed by the preliminary bombardment (see p12). Defences flanking Sausage and Mash Valleys were to be destroyed by the Lochnagar and Y-Sap mines (**Y** on map). The attack, across wide expanses of No Man's Land up valleys between German-held spurs, would have been suicidal without the destruction of those formidable defences.

However, those German defences were not destroyed (see p13), the soldiers springing up from dug-outs and cellars to set up machine-guns with which they cut down the advancing British troops. The scale of the British effort to take La Boisselle and Ovillers was thus matched by the size of the disaster in their failure to do so. The valleys were filled with dead and dying - for very little gain. 34th Div's. casualties, 2500 dead and 3500 wounded, were the highest on July 1st, with 8th Div. close behind. A German soldier's eye-witness account of 8th Div's. assault on Ovillers helps explain the disastrous outcome of the British attack there, and on most sectors of the Somme front, on July 1st:

> The intense bombardment was realized ... to be the prelude to an infantry assault. The men in the dug-outs therefore waited ready, ... At 7.30 a.m. the hurricane of shells ceased as suddenly as it had begun. Our men at once clambered up the steep shafts leading from the dug-outs. ...The machine-guns were .. hurriedly placed in position. ...a series of extended lines of infantry were seen moving forward from the British trenches. The front line appeared to continue without end to right and left. It was quickly followed by a second line, then a third and fourth. They came on at a steady easy pace as if expecting to find nothing alive in our front trenches. "Get ready!" was passed along our front.. A few moments later, when the leading British line was within a hundred yards the rattle of machine-gun fire broke out along the whole line. Red rockets sped up into the blue sky as a signal to our artillery, and immediately afterwards a mass of shells from the German batteries .. burst among the advancing lines. Whole sections seemed to fall... The advance rapidly crumpled under this hail of shells and bullets. All along the line men could be seen throwing up their arms and collapsing, never to move again.

From *Die Schwaben an der Ancre* by M.Gerster, quoted in Volume V of the 'Official History of the War', compiled by Br.Gen. Sir James Edmonds.

Fricourt, July 1st 1916 :-

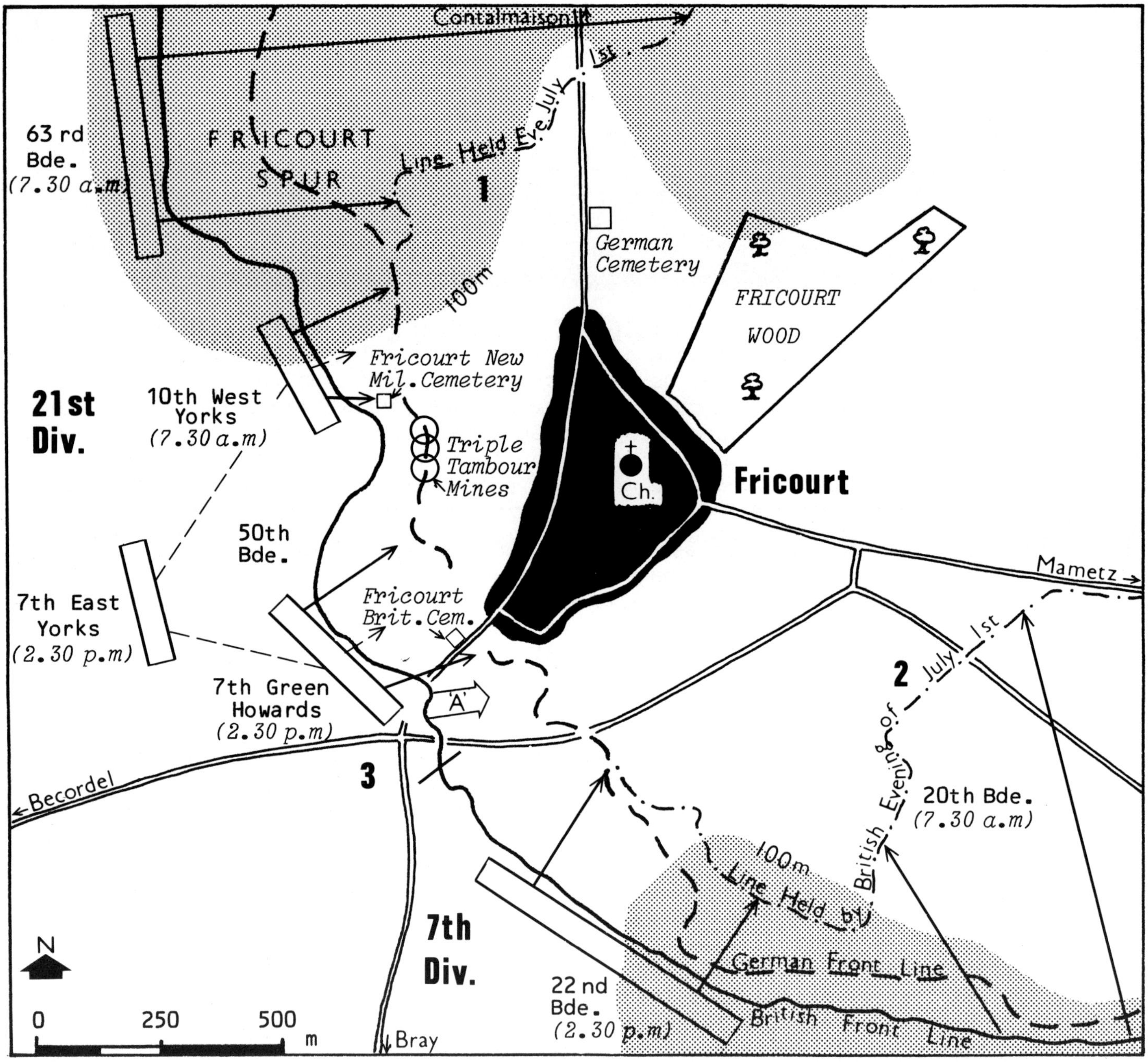

The Tambour, *opposite the north-west side of Fricourt, was where three mines were exploded under the German front line at 7.28 a.m. on July 1st 1916, hence the name 'Triple Tambour', where the craters can be seen today. The German-held village of Fricourt stood at the turning point in the 'L'-shaped British sector of the Somme front (map p4). Because of this, it was decided to take Fricourt by a flanking movement, from the north-west (1 on map; the mines being part of this attack) and from the south-east (2), thus hoping to avoid the need for a direct attack from the south-west (3).*

Fricourt New Military Cemetery *embodies the disaster that befell the 10th West Yorks at 7.30 a.m. on July 1st 1916. The two leading companies crossed No Man's Land with little loss, taking advantage of the barrage and the Tambour mines. However, by the time the other companies advanced the Germans had emerged from their dug-outs and cellars mowing the W.Yorks down with machine-gun fire from Fricourt and Tambour. Their C.O., Lt.Col. A.Dickson, lies with his men in the cemetery, situated in No Man's Land where they fell on that morning.*

The greater effectiveness of the preliminary bombardment from Fricourt Spur eastwards to Maricourt led to the attacks there being more successful than those from Fricourt Spur northwards to Serre (map p4). Casualties were high in the south too, but destruction of German dug-outs, and better wire-cutting and counter-battery work, allowed more success on July 1st (p26-29). Being at the boundary of these two situations, the attack on Fricourt met with mixed fortunes. The attack on Fricourt Spur by the 63rd and 64th Brigades of the 21st Division was reasonably successful (1 on map), as was that by the 20th Brigade of the 7th Division from the south-east (2). However, despite the bombardment and the Tambour mines, the fortifications in and around Fricourt village itself were intact. This is why the 10th West Yorks suffered so badly (see above), and why Fricourt was still in German hands in the early afternoon of the 1st of July.

The 22nd Brigade of the 7th Division and part of the 50th Brigade of the 21st Division were detailed to wait until 2.30 p.m. in case a direct attack on Fricourt from the south-west was needed (3). However, by some ghastly mis-judgement, the C.O. of 'A' Company of the 7th Yorkshire Regiment (the Green Howards) had ordered his men to attack Fricourt at 7.45 a.m. (arrow 'A' on map opposite). They were virtually annihilated before going twenty yards. So, at 2.30 p.m. only three companies of the 7th Green Howards, later supported by the 7th East Yorks, went forward. But they too were cut down by German machine-gun fire from Fricourt. The graves of some of these men, and a special memorial to the 7th Green Howards, can be seen in Fricourt British Cemetery, situated in the old No Man's Land where they fell. The attack by 22nd Bde. at 2.30 p.m. was a little more successful, but on the evening of July 1st, Fricourt remained in German hands. However, under threat of being outflanked, the Germans withdrew from Fricourt on July 2nd.

The German Cemetery *is by the Fricourt-Contalmaison road. The Germans had no organisation like the Imperial War Graves Commission in 1918 (p3), and many of the German dead were never recovered from the Somme battlefield. Some that were are collected together here, buried beneath metal crosses sometimes bearing four names, about 5000 men lying in this stark, sombre place. From the cemetery it is possible to look up onto Fricourt Spur to the west where the struggle to take Fricourt, including the ill-fated attack by the W.Yorks, took place.*

Mametz, July 1st 1916:-

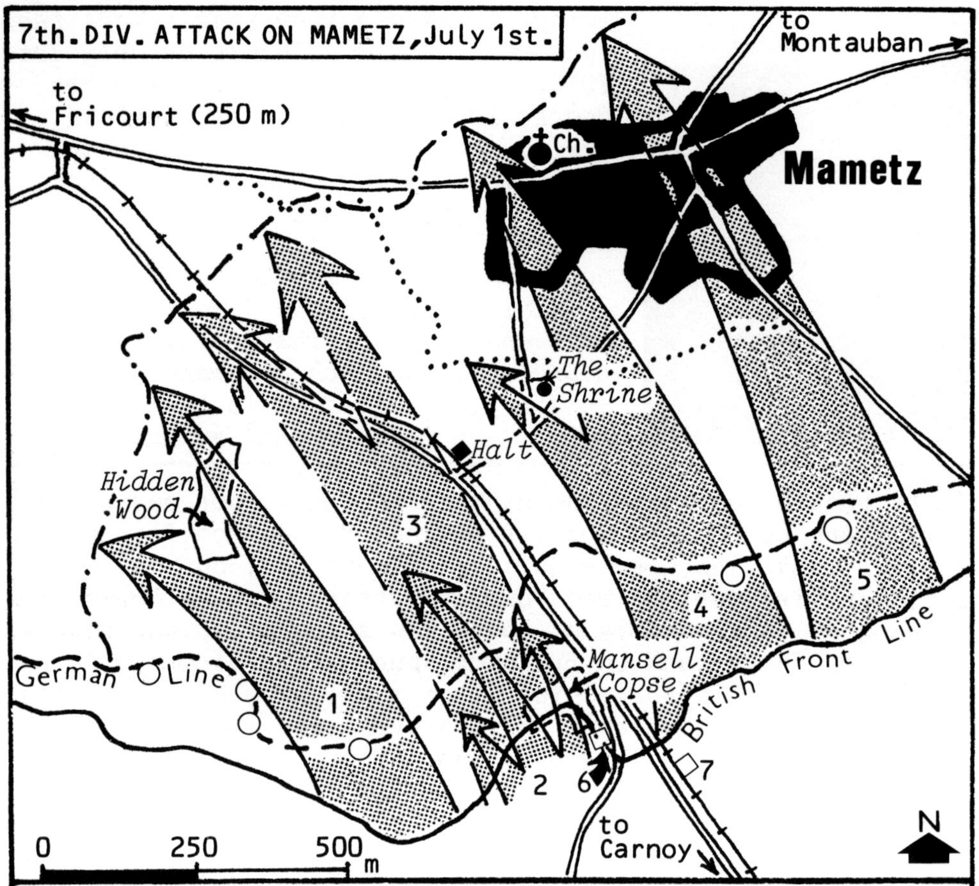

British Front, 7.30 a.m. ——— *German Front, 7.30 a.m.* — — —
German Intermediate Line .... *(for village defence)*
Line reached by British troops, evening July 1st —·—·—·—
Small mines blown 7.28 a.m. ○ *roads* ═══ *railway* ┼┼┼┼
1 *2nd Borderers* 2 *9th Devons* 3 *8th Devons (supporting 9th)*
4 *2nd Gordon Highlanders* 5 *1st South Staffordshires*
6 *Devonshire Cemetery (*Martin and Hodgson*)* 7 *Gordon Cemetery*

The 7th Division's task was to capture the village of Mametz and thus to 'threaten' Fricourt from the south-east, helping in the plan to force the Germans out of that village (see p24-25). By the end of the afternoon Mametz had been captured, but at the cost of considerable casualties (see map for details of battalion advances). German machine-gun posts were the main problem. Some were in the ruins of the village, and some just to the south of it, e.g. at *The Shrine* in the village cemetery. Some of these casualties are in Gordon Cemetery (7 on map) where men of the 2nd Gordon Highlanders lie near the front line from which they advanced at 7.30 a.m. on that misty morning in 1916 (arrow 4 on the map indicates the line of their advance). Like most of the villages that were attacked on July 1st, Mametz was just ruins. It has been rebuilt, and it is also possible to visit the old *Shrine* site today.

German machine-gun post *in a ruined village similar to how those in Mametz must have looked on July 1st 1916.* (IWM Q 23935)

Mansell Copse *seen from the 'Shrine' position in Mametz village cemetery. The German machine-gunners had a clear view of the 9th Devons as they advanced from left to right along the far side of the Carnoy-Fricourt valley. This is precisely what Capt. Martin of the Devons predicted (see opposite).*

Lt. William N. Hodgson MC, 9th Devons

I, that on my familiar hill
Saw with uncomprehending eyes
A hundred of Thy sunsets spill
Their fresh and sanguine sacrifice,
Ere the sun swings his noonday sword
Must say good-bye to all of this;-
By all delights that I shall miss,
Help me to die, O Lord.

The final verse of Before Action *written by W.N. Hodgson on June 29th 1916. (photo. by Langfier)*

Despite the relative success of the 7th Division attack on Mametz, the 9th Devons suffered very badly. The *Official History of the War* (Vol.V: *Edmonds 1932*) states that:

> From the moment its first lines entered No Man's Land, they suffered from a devastating machine-gun barrage, their movement being completely exposed to direct fire. ...Fully half the casualties of the battalion occured before Mansell Copse in the centre of No Man's Land ...was reached.

After only ten minutes of the attack all of the Devon's officers and many of the men had been cut down. Two of those officers were Capt.D.L.Martin and Lt.W.N.Hodgson MC. While home on leave Capt.Martin had made a plasticine model of the area over which the company he commanded was to advance on July 1st (see arrows 2 on map). He predicted that they would be exposed to fire from the German machine-gun posts, especially if such a post was located at *The Shrine* in Mametz village cemetery. No one seems to have heeded his warning because it turned out to be correct in every detail and had the consequences he predicted. Capt.Martin lies with the men he commanded in Devonshire Cemetery (see 6 on map). William Noel Hodgson MC was bombing officer in the 9th Devons. He was a poet, and obviously had the same feeling as Capt.Martin that July 1st 1916 was to be the last day of his life. On the eve of the attack he wrote a poem called *Before Action*, in the last verse of which he shows that he believed he would die in the attack, even predicting that it would be *Ere the sun swings his noonday sword* (see above). He also lies in Devonshire Cemetery near where he fell on July 1st 1916.

Devonshire Cemetery *is situated on the old British front line at the edge of Mansell Copse. It was near here that the 9th Devons formed-up at 7.30 a.m. on July 1st, only moments before being mown down by German machine-guns. These men, and some of the 8th Devons sent in to continue the attack, were buried in the old front trench, a notice proclaiming that* The Devonshires held this trench: The Devonshires hold it still. *They do so still.*

Montauban, July 1st 1916:-

It was the task of 30th Div. to take Montauban on July 1st, while 18th Div. were to take the ridge that ran from the village towards Mametz. The reason both Divisions achieved these objectives was largely because the preliminary bombardment came close to doing what it was meant to do (see p12); Allied superiority in numbers of guns and good spotting of the German batteries being the main reason for this. Counter-battery work was particularly successful, wire-cutting had been quite effective and large parts of the German trenches had been destroyed. Even some of the dug-outs in Montauban itself had been damaged. So, the advance at 7.30 a.m. was successful, especially on the 30th Div. front where they had to pause to wait for their own 'creeping barrage' (see p13) to lift off the German support trenches. Unfortunately, there were some deadly hold-ups caused by isolated, but strongly fortified, German machine-gun posts (e.g. x, y, and z on the map) that had survived the bombardment. These held up the left of the 30th Div., pinned the 7th Queens down for most of the morning and inflicted heavy casualties on the 8th East Surreys (see Capt. Nevill opposite). They also caused the reserve battalions problems, including the 7th West Kents, when they first advanced later in the morning (see below). However, Montauban was taken, by the 90th Brigade of 30th Div., at about 10.00 a.m., and the line beyond the village and along the ridge towards Mametz by between 11.00 a.m. and noon. The British troops could have gone further, as German reinforcements were slow to come up, but there were no strategic plans for this. The success at Montauban showed the importance of an effective preliminary bombardment in an infantry attack, and stood in marked contrast to most sectors of the front north of Fricourt Spur in this respect.

The waiting was over for Frank Bastable

and his comrades in the 7th West Kents on July 1st 1916. They were no longer just 'holding the line', the time had come to attack not defend. Though held in reserve at first, they were soon needed to relieve the beleaguered 7th Queens and 8th East Surreys. Frank recalls July 1st:

It was a misty morning, but this soon cleared when the sun came right up - lovely day it was later on. Yes, we felt tense, but this is what we'd waited for - for a year now. To know we were at last 'going over the top' was a sort of relief. In a way we were frightened and excited at the same time. That last barrage was terrible - just before zero, I'd never heard a noise like it. Montauban our objective was, you could see it on the ridge. We had a drop of rum - Dutch courage I suppose. Well, they really had us pinned down at first, you couldn't stand up, you had to crawl. You could hear the rattle of the machine-guns. Our Sergeant-Major, Button his name was, he stood up - I remember because I was right next to him - and put his stick up for us to follow, but he didn't stand a chance. He got killed almost straight away; he should have got a medal that bloke. Anyway, we got forward by crawling - we were surprised to find that the Germans had gone when we got to their trenches. We got on better after that. I remember it being hot, lying there and getting really thirsty. Well, we got through in the end and took our objective - I don't think many did that day, we were one of the few. I was lucky really.

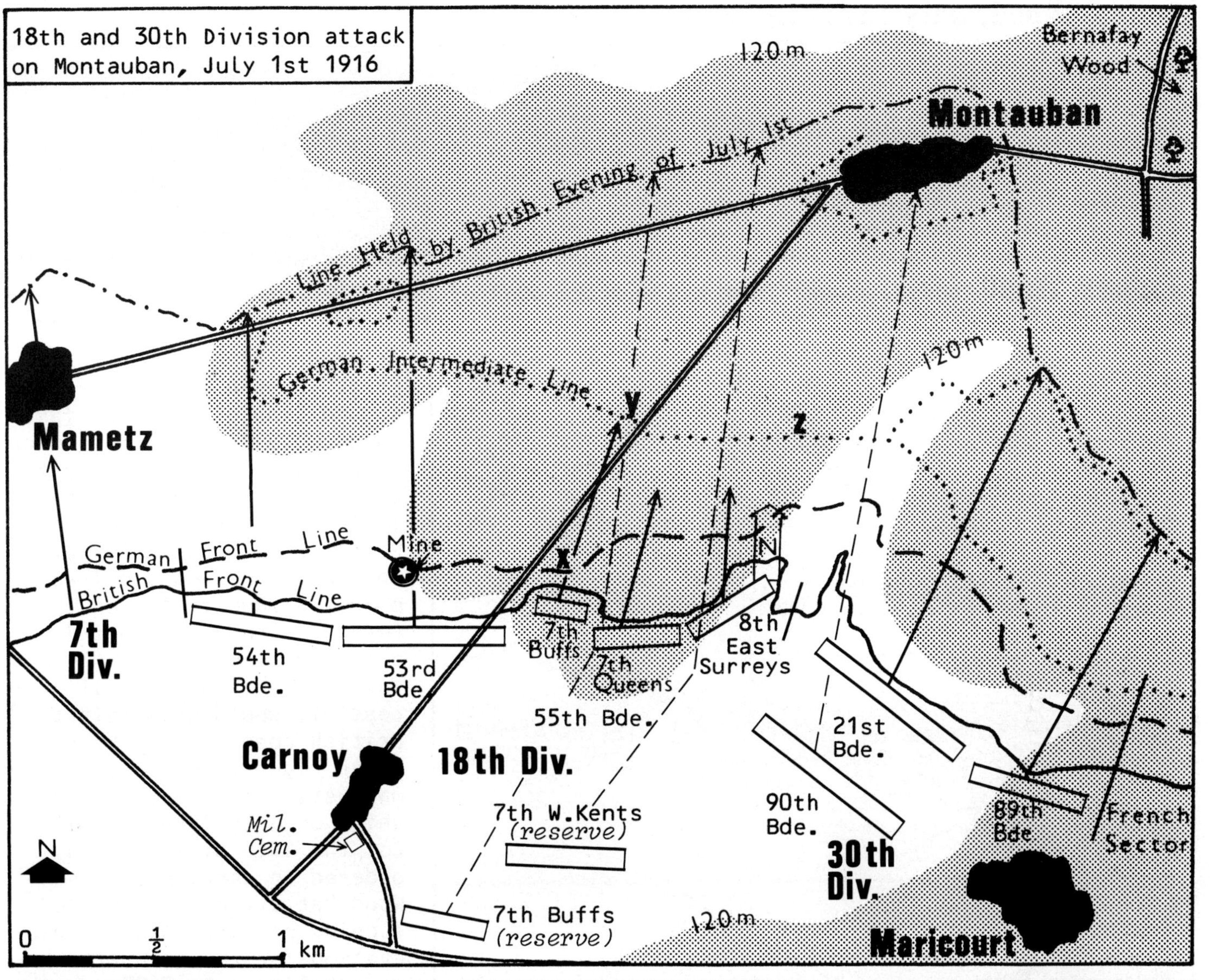

Capt.W.P. Nevill, *a company commander attached to the 8th East Surreys, thought of an original way to encourage his men to go forward at zero hour on July 1st. He gave each of his four platoons a football, the idea being that they would compete to see which one would be the first to dribble their football up to the German front line. However, as explained on the opposite page, the 8th East Surreys were badly held up by the German machine-gun fire and suffered heavy casualties. They lost nearly all their officers (arrow* N *on the map represents Capt.Nevill's advance). As the* Horley Advertiser *for July 29th 1916 described, under the heading 'AN HISTORIC FOOTBALL':-*

> An interesting ceremony took place at the Barracks at Kingston-on-Thames, the headquarters of the East Surrey Regiment, on Friday, at a special parade in the barrack square, the occasion being the formal reception of a football which one of the battalions dribbled into action in the great advance on July 1st. ...As was now well known the battalion was led out of the British trenches by Captain Nevill, and the signal for the advance was given by his kicking off this football. With splendid gallantry ... this and other footballs were dribbled, under a withering fire, right up to the German trenches. ....At no small cost had that football been dribbled up to the German trenches. The officer who kicked it off fell himself in front of the German trenches.

Captain Nevill's grave can be seen in the Military Cemetery at Carnoy (see map above), his headstone bearing the name of his original East Yorkshire Regiment. Leaving July 1st, we shall now look at some of the later events of the First Battle of the Somme.

Trones Wood, July 13/14th 1916:-

Trones Wood *today, viewed from the eastern edge of Bernafay Wood.*

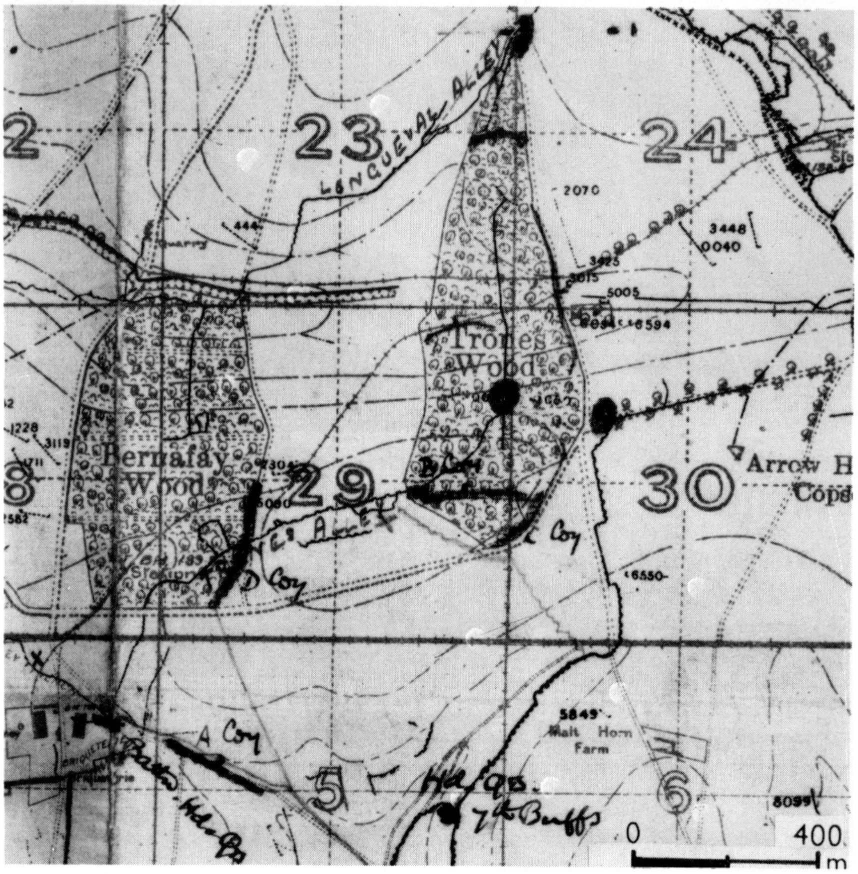

Trench map, *included in the War Diary of the 7th Bn. West Kents, which was used during their attack on Trones Wood. Battalion H.Q. is shown at the Briqueterie (brick works), and the deployment of the Companies is shown, e.g. 'C' company at the southern edge of the wood. The black blobs are the German strong-points.*
(By permission of Controller of H.M.S.O.; PRO WO 95/2049)

Although the Allied plan to break through to the German Second Line of Defences failed on July 1st 1916 (see page 14-29), by July 13th the British were close to this line in the southern part of their Somme front between Bernafay Wood and Contalmaison (see p4-5). A dawn attack on the German Second Line in this area was planned for July 14th. However, such a move, if successful, would have left the British open to attack on their right flank if the Germans still held Trones Wood, which on July 13th they did. So the 18th Division was ordered to capture Trones Wood "at all costs" on the evening of July 13th in preparation for the main attack on the 14th. At 7.00 p.m. the 7th Queens attacked the northern tip of Trones Wood, while the 7th Buffs (the usual name for the East Kent Regiment) and the 7th West Kents, including Frank Bastable in 'C' company, entered it from the south (see map opposite and photograph below). Frank was to be wounded for the first time (see opposite page).

Southern *edge of Trones Wood, where 'C' company of the 7th West Kents entered the wood on the evening of July 13th 1916. The memorial by the wood is that to the 18th Division, who also fought for the wood in 1918. Once in the wood they met* "determined resistance" *from the Germans, and extremely* "dense undergrowth".

Inside Trones Wood, *showing the dense undergrowth in 1916.* (IWM Q 861)

Walking wounded *at an advanced dressing station, Bernafay Wood, July 1916.* (IWM Q 811)

Frank Bastable, of the 7th West Kents, recalls what it was like in Trones Wood on the night of July 13th 1916:

> You could hardly move, the undergrowth was so thick. You couldn't dig-in because of the tree roots, you just couldn't get through them. We had to lie down as close to the ground as we could, but the bullets were coming along level with the ground, a few inches up - that's how I got hit in the top of the shoulder. I knew I had to get out, but it was difficult to find the way. I managed it in the end, but I had to climb over a lot of dead chaps. Terrible it was.

As Frank suggests, many of the 7th West Kents did not get out of Trones Wood alive that night because of the ferocity of the German resistance. The 7th Queens and 7th Buffs suffered a similar fate. When midnight came and the wood was still in German hands the 12th Middlesex and 6th Northamptons (also of the 18th Division) were sent in. They managed to collect up some of the men of the original attacking battalions, including the West Kents, and eventually they formed a line abreast and relentlessly worked their way northwards through the mass of trees and undergrowth, driving the Germans before them. Many men died, but Trones Wood was in British hands shortly after the main attack on the German Second Line started in the early hours of July 14th.

Trones Wood has recovered from the ravages of war today, and its undergrowth is as dense as in 1916. These much fought over trees are as unwelcoming today as they were then.

Bernafay Wood Cemetery *(see map p6) contains the grave of Pte.Spencer Gatland of the 7th West Kents, who died in the attack on Trones Wood on July 13th 1916. (The Cemetery Register tells us that he came from Maidstone). A few feet from his grave is that of Pte.A.Austin, also of the 7th West Kents, who died on August 27th 1918, when Trones Wood had to be taken all over again in the British offensive during the Second Battle of the Somme.*

Delville Wood, July 15th to Sept. 1916:-

In September 1916 *Delville Wood was no more than shattered stumps intermingled with trench-lines. This was the result of an almost continuous bombardment, by both sides, since mid-July when the fierce struggle for the wood began. Even the broad rides, named after London, Capetown and Edinburgh streets were no longer discernable.* (IWM Q 4267)

Today *the wood has been replanted and the original rides re-established, with stone markers bearing their old names (see map). Only the preserved trench lines indicate that this now peaceful wood was once the scene of so much death and destruction between July and September 1916.*

Longueval and Delville Wood stood at the turning point in the southern part of the British front on July 14th 1916 (see map p4), the line running west to Ovillers and south to the newly-won Trones Wood. The possession of Delville Wood, being seen as the key to the taking of Guillemont, Ginchy, High Wood, and eventually Flers, was ordered to be taken 'at all costs' on July 15th. Attacking woods presents special problems. If you enter one part while the enemy is in another it is difficult for either side initially to shell in support for fear of killing their own men. However, if you succeed in taking all or some distinct parts of the wood the enemy can organise a barrage that will help drive you out. Because this state of affairs actually materialized, Delville Wood, or parts of it, changed hands a number of times between July 15th and early September 1916, when it eventually fell to the British. But in the meantime the wood had been pulverised by the intensive bombardment by both sides in the struggle for its possession.

It was the South African Brigade that first attempted to take Delville Wood on July 15th. Following a very effective dawn bombardment of the wood, they quickly cleared the southern half and took the rest, except the north-west corner, during the rest of the day. Digging-in, through tree roots and mangled wood, proved as difficult as the 7th W.Kents had found in Trones Wood. The German shelling, machine-gun fire and counter-attacks now started - the problems of possessing such an easy target as a wood had begun!. Attempts to take the north-west corner on the 16th and 17th failed, and on both nights the S.African soldiers endured intense shelling, including gas shells. On the 18th the Germans launched a major counter-attack and the S.Africans, engaged in fierce fighting, were forced back to Buchanan Street (see map). A small detachment hung on in the extreme south-east corner of the wood until the 19th. Late on the 20th of July the S.Africans were at last relieved, but the six days of heroic endurance in Delville Wood had cost them dear. They went in on the 15th with 121 Officers and 3032 Men, and emerged on the 20th with only 29 Officers and 751 Men. This is why it is proper that Delville Wood is preserved in their memory today. However, on July 20th 1916, the Germans still occupied most of Delville Wood.

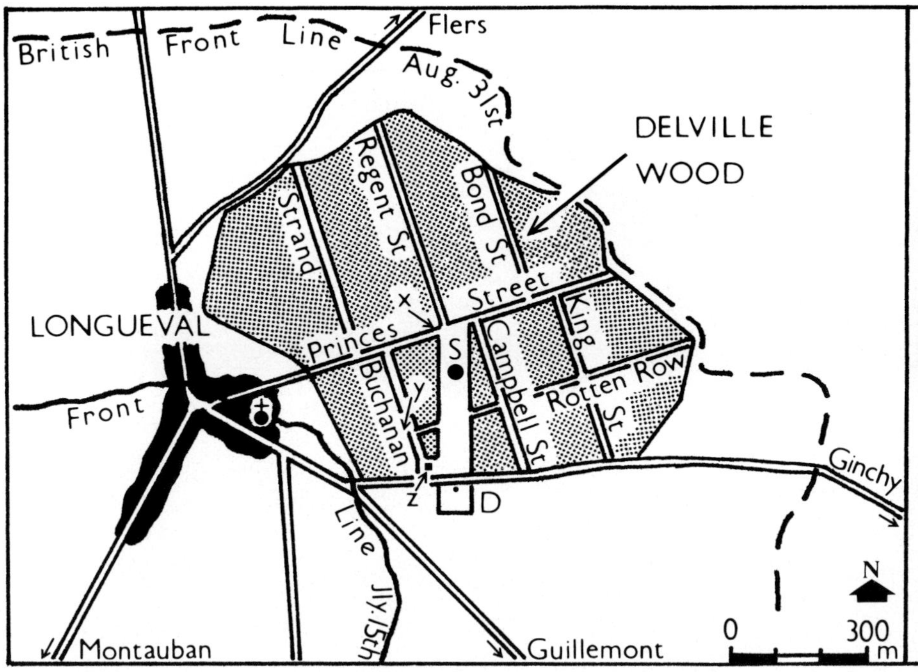

A second attempt to take Delville Wood was made on July 27th by the 99th Brigade of the 2nd Div. It was now the German's turn to suffer under a bombardment, following which the 99th made good progress, taking all of the wood except the northern edge by 9.00 a.m. But once in British hands, the German shelling of the wood began, and they launched a counter-attack at 9.30 a.m. The 'Official History' records that the Brigade's machine-guns were "handled with boldness" (see Capt. Grant below), and the 99th held on until the 29th, but were still unable to dislodge the Germans from the northern part of the wood. In attacks on the 18th and 25th of August, 14th Div. finally cleared the wood, though a German counter-attack retook the eastern edge for a few days. So it had taken until early September to carry out the order of July 15th to take Delville Wood,'at all costs'.

The South African Memorial, indeed the whole of Delville Wood, commemorates not just those who died here in July 1916, but all of the 10,000 S.Africans who died in the First World War. One of the original trees of the wood remains (x on map), and by one of the re-established rides, Buchanan Street, the site of the S.African Brigade H.Q. of July 1916 is marked (y on map). Do not stray from the grassy rides, even to explore old trench lines, advice and guidance being available from the Warden's house (z on map).

Capt. C.B. Grant *commanded a machine-gun section of the 99th Bde., and died in their attack on Delville Wood on July 27th (see above). His home was near where I presently live, and I discovered that the local newspaper, the* West Sussex County Times, *contained details of his death in the edition for August 12th 1916. Printed in the paper were letters recently received by Capt. Grant's mother. One was from 2nd Lt. C. Stone, who had been with Capt. Grant in Delville Wood on the 27th:*

> .. a terrible day, and place, and all who were there spoke in glowing terms of Captain Grant, who was here, there, and everywhere, helping everyone, unperturbed and cool as ever, although he knew before he started that it was almost certain death. .. of his nine or ten officers, only one came back. Captain Grant was beloved by all the Battalion. He combined extraordinary ability in his work with a wonderful coolness in danger.. I needn't tell you what a fine and gallant fellow he was.

Flers-Courcelette, September 1916:-

Mark 1 Tank *during the Flers-Courcelette battle, Sept.1916* (IWM Q 2489)

An attempt to break through the German defences between Thiepval and Combles was planned for Sept.15th 1916. But how was the deadly German machine-gun fire to be overcome?. The answer, it was hoped, would be the 'tank', designed to go ahead of the infantry and clear a path for them. Called tanks because their true purpose was initially hidden behind the pretence that they were water carriers, it was planned to unveil this new weapon on the front between Flers and Courcelette on Sept.15th. Although individual tanks proved useful on the day, they were too few in number, mechanically unreliable, unable to cope with the shell-cratered landscape and, above all, slow. They either became easy targets for German shells or the infantry soon got ahead of them. So the infantry made the gains on Sept.15th mainly in the usual way, i.e. against unequal odds, and the hoped for breakthrough did not occur. Some people complained that the secret of the tank had been revealed too early in 1916, before proper tactics for its use had been worked out.

Tank Corps memorial, *including this model Mark V 'male' tank, on the line from which the first tanks used in war advanced on September 15th 1916. (The model is c.1 m long)*

Canadian memorial *marking the line to which the Canadian Divisions advanced, including the capture of the village of Courcelette, on Sept15th 1916.*

High Wood *lay before the 47th(London) Div. on Sept. 15th 1916. Because the German lines were so close to the British it was not possible to bombard them before the attack. Four tanks were allotted to make up for this, but two could not even get through the tree stumps in the wood, diverting to the open where one lost direction and the other got stuck in a shell-hole. The one that did get forward was hit by a shell and set on fire. The Londoners were thus badly cut-up by machine-gun fire until a mortar barrage later in the morning helped them clear the wood. Near the London Div. memorial (opposite; leaning due to subsidence) is London Cemetery which includes men of the 47th Div. killed on Sept.15th in plot 1A.*

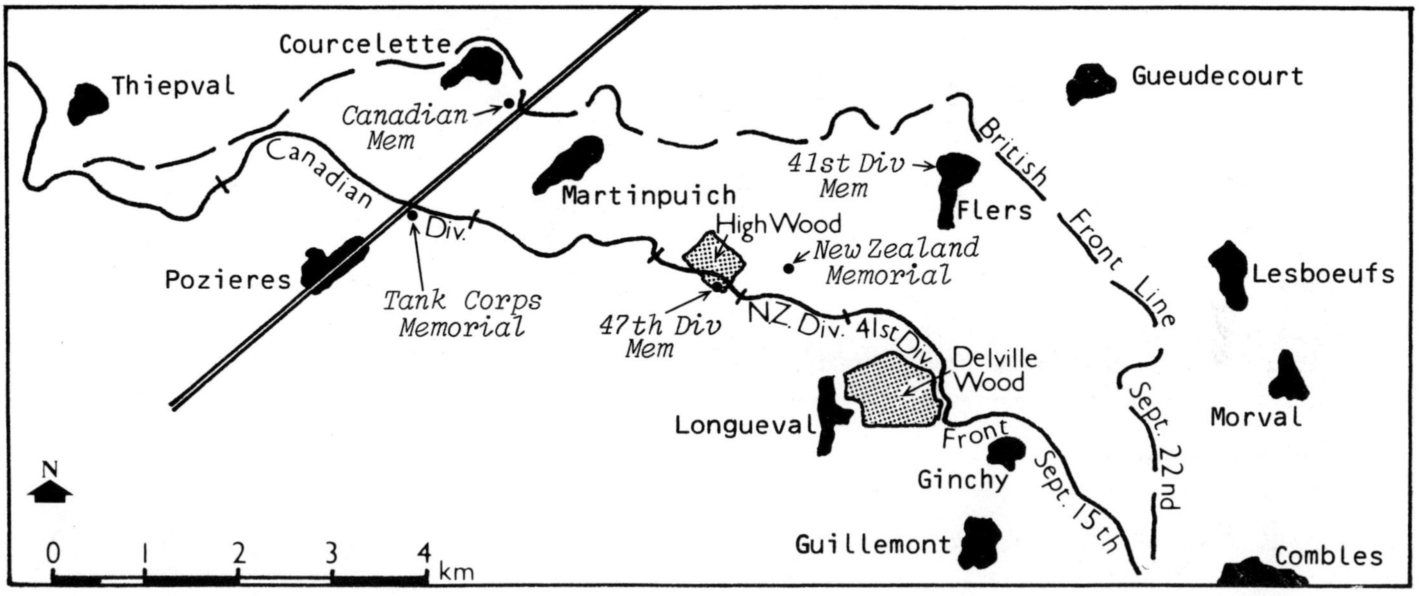

The winter of 1916 was severe, soldiers of both sides suffering from that common enemy, the weather. Attempts to break through the German defences north of Thiepval in Nov.1916 were nearly cancelled because of the muddy conditions. Although the attack on Beaumont-Hamel succeeded (p15 and 18), the battle for Serre on Nov.13th was 'lost in the mud'. The photograph shows the conditions on the Somme battlefield in Nov.1916. This is the Lesboeufs 'road' near Flers *(IWM Q 2980)*. It has been said that the First Battle of the Somme just petered out into the mud of mid-Nov. 1916, the 'season' for offensive warfare apparently being over for that year. Both Frank Bastable and Kirby Pain (see p37) of the 7th West Kents remember the intense cold which took over from the rain in December 1916. In his memoirs Kirby Pain wrote:

> Just before Christmas we had a heavy fall of snow and then it froze solidly for over 6 weeks. During this cold period Gerry made good his retreat back behind the devastated area and so shortened his lines ... it was now well into Feb.1917.

German retreat to the Hindenburg Line, spring 1917:-

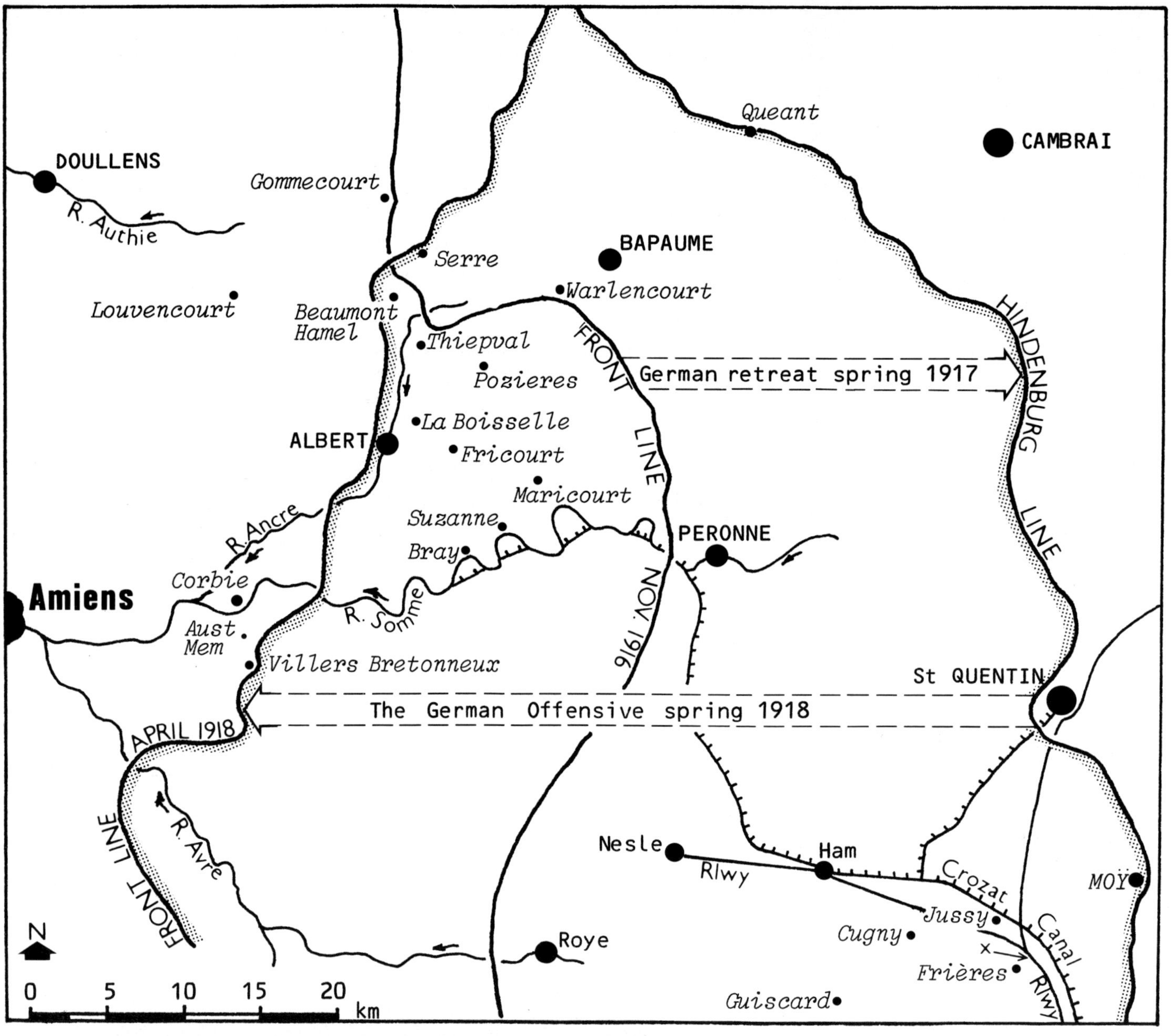

In February 1917 *the Germans began to retreat from the Somme front. But this was a tactical decision by them, to make their overall position on the Western Front more secure, not a victory for the Allies. The ground that had been so bitterly contested was now there for the taking. These men are in Serre, at last given up by the Germans – it never was taken in battle. But their smiles disappeared when they saw the carefully prepared, fortress-like, line of defences to which the Germans had retreated – the* Hindenburg Line. *The daunting task of trying to take yet another German line of defences was about to begin.* (IWM Q 1788)

German advance, spring 1918 :-

Retreating British soldiers, *carrying a wounded comrade, pass through an Allied outpost 'covering' their withdrawal near Roye, March 25th 1918. Just four days earlier, on March 21st, relieved of pressure on their Eastern Front resulting from the Russian Revolution of 1917, the Germans had begun a massive offensive. They swept westwards to near Amiens in a matter of days (see map opposite). They retook the old Somme battlefield of 1916, the British having to fight for it again in 1918.* (IWM Q 10824)

V.K. Pain joined the 7th Bn. Royal West Kents (18th Div) in Sept. 1914, the same battalion as Frank Bastable, and, like Frank, Kirby Pain found himself 'holding the Somme line' in 1915-16. Then he was asked to be clerk to the new 18th Div. School of Instruction near Corbie. So in March 1918 Kirby was working at the Reinforcement and Training Camp near Cugny, and his old battalion, the 7th West Kents, were at the front near by, opposite the Hindenburg Line at Moÿ. Their battalion War Diary for March 20th 1918 records that they were told to 'stand to' as the "enemy was massing in large numbers". For the 21st the entry begins: "Under cover of dense mist enemy advanced". The German Spring Offensive of 1918 had thus begun, the Allied Front Defences being quickly penetrated. Reinforcements were sent for and Kirby Pain found himself in the thick of the fighting.

Awakened by the German bombardment at 4.30 a.m. on March 21st, Kirby realized that this was 'It'. His company was marched to a position by a railway embankment just west of the Crozat Canal (see x on map). Seeing remnants of 18th Div. moving back it soon became obvious that "things had gone badly". On the 22nd, short of supplies, guns and ammunition, Kirby's company could see the Germans massing on the other side of the canal - the 'crunch' was about to come. Early on the 23rd his C.O. was killed by a shell and, as Kirby relates in his memoirs, the Adjutant took charge and:

> .. just as dawn was breaking he ordered all of us to the top of the embankment and be prepared to fire as soon as Gerry poked his head over the other side as he said he was certain the Bosche had got across the canal during the night. It was not a pleasant thought that the first sight of Gerry would be only 15 yards away. It was difficult to keep your head up to be prepared to fire as they had machine-guns traversing up and down the top of the embankment. Just as it was getting a little lighter... I turned round to see a company of East Surreys from our Division had come to relieve us. Was I glad! but I felt sorry for those poor devils as I guessed that they would all be killed or taken prisoner before long. I learned afterwards that ... they did mostly get taken prisoner before 9.00 a.m.

Kirby then went on to describe, in his memoirs and to me personally, how they had to withdraw westwards quite rapidly and in considerable confusion "as the Bosche was still pressing forward", until in early April "Haig issued his famous order to 'stand fast in front of Amiens'." And that was, in fact, where the Germans were halted.

'Second Somme', summer 1918:-

Australian Memorial *and the British Military Cemetery near Villers Bretonneux, 15 km east of Amiens (map p36). Villers Bretonneux was the furthest west the Germans got in their advance on Amiens in 1918, the Demarcation Stone on the eastern edge of the village reminding us of this fact (photo. p5). The Germans did capture the village on April 23rd 1918, but on the following day, helped by the 8th and 18th Divs, the 4th and 5th Australian Divisions recaptured it. Then, on August 8th 1918, "the black day of the German army" as Ludendorff, Germany's Chief of Staff, called it, the 2nd and 5th Australian Divisions advanced from the eastern outskirts of Villers Bretonneux at the start of the Allied Offensive which eventually pushed the Germans back for the last time. It is for this reason that the Australian National War Memorial overlooks Villers Bretonneux and why the village was 'adopted' by the city of Melbourne, the school being rebuilt in 1923 from funds raised by the children of Victoria. The Memorial was damaged during the Second World War and, although restored, the superficial scars have been left, as a plaque informs us, "for the purposes of historical interest". I believe that they are calling upon the visitor to reflect on the capability of Governments to make the same mistakes twice.*

Tanks, artillery, bomber and fighter aircraft, and cavalry worked together on August 8th 1918 in one of the most successful Allied offensives of the war. A preliminary bombardment of the 1916 type (p 12), which did little except warn the Germans of an impending attack, was not used. Priority was given to maintaining the element of surprise. On the day itself the battle opened with a creeping barrage of a more continuous type, i.e. less 'step-like' than in 1916 (p 13), and it was to assist in the advance of a spear-head of heavy tanks rather than infantry alone. Developments in the tanks themselves, and their more appropriate use, i.e. in large numbers (over 400 were used in the attack) over less devastated and dry ground, was one of the main factors in the Allied success on August 8th. The large Mark V tanks (see photo. of model p34) and most of all the new lighter and faster Whippet tanks were much more effective in 1918 than their predecessors of 1916 (though still prone to breakdown). The newly named RAF used bombers to attack the German supply and communication lines and low-flying fighters strafed the German trenches (one of their main rivals, Baron von Richthofen, having been shot down near Corbie in April). The cavalry, reminder of an older-style warfare, were able to follow through the attack. So, by nightfall on August 8th the Allies had advanced by up to 9 km on the front between the River Avre and the River Ancre.

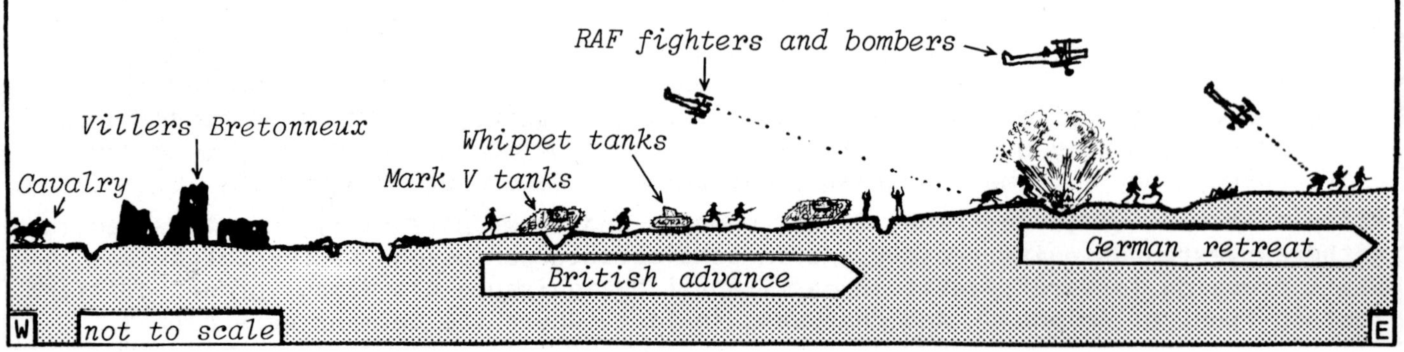

Lt. J. Brillant VC, MC,

of the 22nd Canadien Francais Battalion, was part of the Canadian force that joined the Australians in launching the Allied Offensive on August 8th 1918. He died on the third day of the advance, and in so doing won the Victoria Cross. He lies in the British Cemetery at Villers Bretonneux, by the Australian Memorial. Although every soldier is important, the Cemetery Register (p 3) gives much more information about VC holders than others. It does this by including an extract from the London Gazette where the reasons for the award of the medal are given. In Lt.Brillant's case the extract from the Gazette for Sept.27th 1918 reads:

> For most conspicuous bravery and outstanding devotion to duty when in charge of a company which he led in attack during two days with absolute fearlessness and extraordinary ability and initiative, the extent of the advance being twelve miles.

It goes on to describe how Lt.Brillant was wounded three times in those two days before "he fell unconscious from exhaustion and lack of blood".

Across the Somme battlefield again:

The pace of the Allied advance south of the River Somme soon slowed, the tanks being unable to sustain a long-distance advance. So, in August and September 1918, the old British Somme battlefield of 1916 was fought for again in the 'Second Battle of the Somme'. Though generally in retreat, German resistance cost the lives of many British soldiers, evidence of which can be seen in the Somme cemeteries. The example of the 7th West Kent graves for August 27th 1918 in Bernafay Wood Cemetery is mentioned on p31, resulting from their having to attack Trones Wood once again, the same wood in which the Battalion had suffered so badly in July 1916. The old familiar place names also begin to re-appear in Battalion War Diaries. Private O.C.Morris MM, 7th Royal Sussex Regt., is buried in Peronne Road Cem., Maricourt. On the day that he was killed, August 26th 1918, his Battalion's War Diary reads as follows:

> Attack commenced east of Mametz 4.30 a.m. Held up in front of 1st Objective. CO slightly wounded. 2nd Lt.Lavender killed. ..3.00 p.m.Enemy withdrew. Strong patrols sent forward ..contact gained on Montauban-Carnoy Road. *(PRO WO 95/1856)*

At least the Germans were now withdrawing and the end of the war only weeks away. This makes the death of men like Pte.Morris even more sad, so near the end, but he has a friend who still remembers him. Mr.A.F.Gale, now in his eighties, last saw Pte.Morris when they were comrades in the 11th Royal Sussex Regt. during the Third Battle of Ypres in Nov.1917. He told me about him, as we sat in a café in Ypres, and he was then able to travel to see Pte.Morris's grave at Maricourt in the summer of 1982. For me, this lent a poignant reality to the phrase *"Gone, but not forgotten"*, which is engraved on many of the headstones in cemeteries on the Somme in France and around Ypres in Belgium.

Conclusion: The Home Front, where disaster struck in 1917 . . . .

The Silvertown disaster: *The remains of the munitions works in east London after the fire and explosion on the night of January 19th 1917. Surrounding factories were destroyed or severely damaged, and whole streets of houses were blown down or left in ruins. 69 people were killed and 400 injured. It was later described as one of the greatest disasters on the 'Home Front' during the war.* (IWM Q 15364)

Mabel Bastable, seen here with her husband Frank (see several previous pages) was, as a schoolgirl, an eye-witness to the Silvertown disaster. She lived near the works as her father was chauffeur to the manager of one of the near-by factories. She recalls that night:

There were shouts of 'Fire!', well, you couldn't miss it, the whole place was lit up! We were all outside looking ... I went upstairs to get a shawl. Suddenly I was downstairs and the house was on top of me. Its funny, but I can't really remember hearing the explosion ... but our house was blown down right enough. My sister Winnie was at the Church Hall, a children's treat of some sort. Anyway, the whole lot was blown down .. she had to help hold the roof up while they got the children out. I remember the old horse was killed, the one that used to come round .. we had to climb over him to get out. We had to walk a long way to find somewhere to put up .. my Mum's sister I think we stayed with. We didn't go up to Silvertown again ... I didn't go to school again, there was no school .... no house, so there was no point. We eventually moved to Sevenoaks with my father's boss, he still drove the car. After that they moved again to Chislehurst .. we went with them, Dad as chauffeur and me as parlour maid. That is where I met Frank .. after the war.. He used to deliver the fish .. so something good came from the disaster, and Frank was lucky, he came home from the war.